RED SOX
IN THE
HALL OF FAME

BOSTON RED SOX

VS.

CHICAGO CUBS

DOUBLEDAY FIELD

Cooperstown, N. Y.

JUNE 13, 1940

OFFICIAL SCORE CARD

A new tradition was born on June 13, 1940, as the inaugural Hall of Fame Game was played between the Boston Red Sox and Chicago Cubs at Doubleday Field in Cooperstown, New York. Although Boston lost 10-9 in the rain-shortened game in front of 3,500 fans, it was led by a young Ted Williams, who hit two home runs. Williams and four of his teammates from that year, Joe Cronin, Bobby Doerr, Jimmie Foxx, and Lefty Grove, would later be inducted into the Baseball Hall of Fame. (David Hickey.)

RED SOX
IN THE
HALL OF FAME

David Hickey and Kerry Keene

ARCADIA
PUBLISHING

Published by Arcadia Publishing
Charleston, South Carolina

Printed in the United States of America

Library of Congress Control Number: 2021949728

For all general information, please contact Arcadia Publishing:
Telephone 843-853-2070
Fax 843-853-0044
E-mail sales@arcadiapublishing.com
For customer service and orders:
Toll-Free 1-888-313-2665

Visit us on the Internet at www.arcadiapublishing.com

*For Richard H. Hickey, my Pop, you will forever be in my thoughts.
I miss and love you and will do my best every day to make you proud.
You will never be forgotten.*

—Love, David

*For my late mother, Shirley McMorrow, who took me to see Ted Williams
making an appearance at a Sears store in the early 1960s and whose Red
Sox yearbooks from that period I studied from cover to cover.*

—Love, Kerry

CONTENTS

ACKNOWLEDGMENTS

A project of this magnitude would not be possible without the help of a very supportive lineup. A heartfelt thanks to the following people for their input and assistance: Sam Hickey for his artistic creativity; Ray Sinibaldi for his insight, numerous suggestions, and resources; Rachael Adams for her patience and editorial support; Danny O'Brien for his annual trek to Cooperstown and photography skills; diehard Red Sox fan Ernie Spadaro for swinging for the fences; Pati and Sox for their unwavering loyalty and companionship; Jeff Ruetsche, acquisitions editor at Arcadia Publishing, for his shared vision for this project; Caitrin Cunningham, senior title manager at Arcadia Publishing, for her professionalism and guidance; the entire staff at Arcadia Publishing; Sara Coffin, curator, Boston Red Sox; Cassidy Lent of the National Baseball Library (NBL); Bill Nowlin; Glenn Stout; the Society for American Baseball Research; baseball-reference.com; fenwaypark100.org; and all the people past and present who shared their love for the Boston Red Sox, its greatest players, and the Baseball Hall of Fame through their lenses. Unless otherwise noted, all images are from author David Hickey's private collection.

INTRODUCTION

The turn of the 20th century brought with it a new baseball league and a new major-league ball team for the city of Boston. In 1901, the franchise that would come to be known as the Red Sox took the field for the first time.

Starting with that very first official game in Baltimore on April 26, the Boston American League team roster included two players who went on to be regarded as all-time greats—the immortal pitcher Cy Young and third baseman/manager Jimmy Collins. Both would be inducted into the yet-to-be-created Baseball Hall of Fame years later, with Young being enshrined in the inaugural class of 1939 and Collins in 1945.

Boston went on to win the first modern World Series in 1903 and added championships in 1912, 1915, 1916, and 1918. The Sox became a New England sports institution before the end of their second decade. One thing that Red Sox teams have had in common throughout the years is the presence of truly great personnel—Cy Young, Tris Speaker, Babe Ruth, Jimmie Foxx, Ted Williams, Carl Yastrzemski, Pedro Martinez, and so many others. The Boston Red Sox have remained one of the jewels in the crown of baseball for more than 100 years while showcasing many of the game's greatest legends throughout history.

In the early 20th century, it was generally accepted that the central New York village of Cooperstown was where the game of baseball originated. In 1934, Cooperstown native Stephen C. Clark, head of the Clark Foundation, pursued an idea to create a baseball museum to increase tourism and boost the local economy. With the eventual input of Major League Baseball, the concept evolved in 1936, and the National Baseball Hall of Fame and Museum was created to honor those who had risen to the highest levels of excellence in various aspects of the game. Longtime baseball writers were assigned the yearly task of voting to elect players to be permanently inducted into the newly created institution. In addition, an Old Timers Committee was formed to vote on executives, managers, and others who pioneered various aspects of the game in its development.

Babe Ruth, who was among the initial five players elected in 1936, spent his first six major-league seasons rising to national fame in a Red Sox uniform. When the hall's construction was completed and it was officially opened in June 1939, Ruth was inducted alongside two former Red Sox players, Cy Young and Tris Speaker, as well as Sox general manager Eddie Collins.

From that day to the present, 42 others who have served the Red Sox franchise as a player, manager, or executive have joined them in Cooperstown. All of those presently enshrined are featured on the following pages. As the 21st century progresses, they will no doubt be followed by many more.

On these pages their stories are remembered and will forever be told and retold. The tale is of one city and of one small town coming together to honor those who are the Red Sox in the Baseball Hall of Fame.

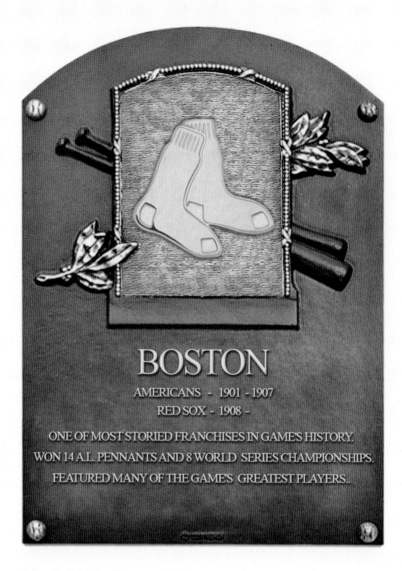

The National Baseball Hall of Fame and Museum in Cooperstown honors the game's greatest players and its most iconic moments. At its heart is the Plaque Gallery, which features bronze plaques of greats who have achieved baseball immortality. Generations of families gaze for hours upon their heroes, recalling memories and emotions only this hallowed room can evoke. Individual teams are not represented with plaques, but if they were, the emotions and love toward those teams would fill the huge hall. Sam Hickey, the author's son, created this realistic painting in 2017 of a Boston Red Sox team plaque to symbolize their stature in the game's history. In 2007, father and son created lifelong memories of their own while coaching and playing together in a weeklong tournament at the baseball village of Cooperstown Dreams Park, just minutes from the hall of fame. Sam, who was 12 years old at the time, wore No. 9 in honor of Ted Williams. (Courtesy of Sam Hickey.)

FOUR SOX FOR THE NEW HALL

It was June 12, 1939, and the baseball season had been underway for two months. Loyal Red Sox fans in Boston and throughout New England were simultaneously focused on the team's current status and its glory days from the distant past. Presently, the team occupied second place in the American League, chasing its rival the New York Yankees. Fans were enjoying watching the development of 20-year-old rookie Ted Williams and up-and-coming star second baseman Bobby Doerr, along with the still-productive twilight years of superstars Jimmie Foxx, Lefty Grove, and shortstop/manager Joe Cronin.

On that same day, 237 miles to the west in the remote central New York village of Cooperstown, four living legends from the Red Sox were being honored for their excellence in an unprecedented ceremony. In the early decades of the 20th century, when a Major League Baseball player achieved an exclusive feat or statistical milestone, sportswriters would often write that he had "made it to the hall of fame," though at the time it was merely a concept. Starting in 1934, the wheels were set in motion to make this idea a reality. The Cooperstown-based Clark Foundation, in conjunction with Major League Baseball, began the process of creating an election system to permanently enshrine honorees periodically. In the initial election held in 1936, the Baseball Writers Association of America (BBWAA) named Ty Cobb, Babe Ruth, Honus Wagner, Christy Mathewson, and Walter Johnson as the first five inductees. Former Red Sox stars Tris Speaker and Cy Young were among eight members added in the 1937 election, and a total of 12 more received the necessary votes in the following two years.

Finally, the National Baseball Hall of Fame and Museum was completed and ready to hold its grand opening, welcoming its first 25 elected members. Ruth, Speaker, Young, and Eddie Collins were among 11 living enshrinees on hand that day to witness the grandest and most legendary event in the history of Cooperstown. The Boston Red Sox would leave an indelible mark on baseball's most historic institution from its very beginning.

This life-sized, three-dimensional display in the Baseball Hall of Fame Museum gives the visitor the feeling that it's alive. All 11 living inductees from the original 25 members, including 4 former Red Sox, attended the inaugural induction ceremony in 1939. The display includes 10 of the 11 players and is missing the great Ty Cobb, who arrived after the picture was taken.

In celebration of baseball's centennial, the Baseball Hall of Fame and Museum opened in June 1939. The day's events consisted of several games at Doubleday Field, a parade down Main Street, and the start of an annual tradition: inducting all-time greats into the newly created shrine. This 24-page grand opening program featured details on the new building, historical information, and pictures of the initial plaques to be displayed.

The tiny central New York village of Cooperstown had a population of around 2,500 in 1939 and had never seen a crowd or an event of this magnitude before. The grand opening of the brand-new National Baseball Hall of Fame and Museum brought a crowd of approximately 12,000 visitors and made the town a destination for all time, with annual pilgrimages to celebrate the enshrinement of the game's greats.

Four years after his final appearance in a major-league game, 44-year-old Babe Ruth is seen here after giving his acceptance speech at the hall of fame's first induction ceremony in 1939. In his speech, Babe referenced his major-league debut 25 years earlier, pitching for the Red Sox on July 11, 1914. Ruth also ended his career in Boston playing for the National League Braves.

The first floor of the original three-story National Baseball Museum is pictured in its very early years. The names of the first 27 inductees were inscribed on one large three-panel plaque that greeted visitors near the entrance. Through the efforts of Stephen Clark, an heir to the Singer Sewing Machine Company, the original 1,200-square-foot museum was built at a cost of $44,000.

To celebrate the opening of the Baseball Hall of Fame and Museum, the US Postal Service issued a postage stamp honoring the game. Pictured is a postcard with the new stamp affixed and postmarked at 9:00 a.m. from the Cooperstown Post Office. Dated June 12, 1939, the day of the first induction ceremony, the postcard was signed by all 11 living inductees.

As part of the inaugural hall of fame induction ceremony in 1939, an exhibition game was played at Doubleday Field. Two players from each of the 16 major-league franchises played on teams captained by Eddie Collins and Honus Wagner. Collins, Red Sox general manager at the time, is seen here in what may have been the only time he wore a Boston uniform.

One of the more prominent figures at the inaugural induction ceremony was 72-year-old pitching great Cy Young. Upon his election in 1937, Young donated the ball from his 500th pitching win to the museum, along with other memorabilia from his career, prompting others to do the same. After the ceremony, he appeared at the Legends Game at Doubleday Field with his fellow inductees in baseball uniforms.

Tris Speaker was among the 11 living inductees at the hall's historic first ceremony. He had been elected to the new shrine in 1937 along with his former Red Sox teammate Cy Young. At that time, nearly seven full decades into the history of Major League Baseball, the "Gray Eagle" was still considered among the top two center fielders in the game's history along with fellow inductee Ty Cobb.

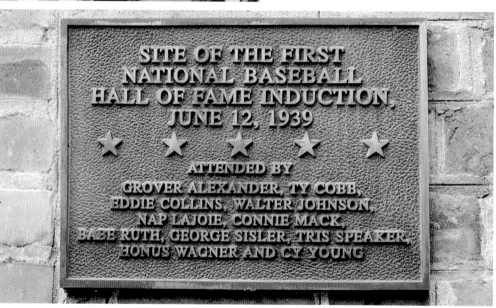

This bronze plaque was placed on the exterior of the Baseball Hall of Fame and Museum to commemorate the historic event held there at its very beginning in 1939. Baseball commissioner Judge Kennesaw Mountain Landis presided over the ceremony, joined by American and National League presidents William Harridge and Ford Frick. These three men would eventually earn plaques of their own in Cooperstown for their contributions to baseball.

THE GALLERY OF
BOSTON STARS GROWS

In recent decades, Boston fans are often referred to as "Red Sox Nation," but at the dawn of the 20th century, they were the "Royal Rooters." They were passionate about Boston baseball played at its highest level and immediately embraced the newly created American League franchise. The team had earned instant credibility by signing two top stars from the rival National League.

Pitcher Cy Young was an ace in the National League for a decade and was still in his prime with many good years ahead. Jimmy Collins was starring at third base for the nearby National League Boston team, and after being lured away, he would excel in the dual role of playing third and managing the new squad on the field. These two original stars led the team to its first world championship two years later and cemented their legacies in the hearts and minds of the city's sports fans. Young and Collins became the first two links in a very long chain of great players in Red Sox history to eventually earn their spot in Cooperstown.

By the early 1920s, team owner Harry Frazee had traded or sold off several links in the hall of fame chain, which directly led to some of the team's darkest days. In spite of that, it still won more world championships by 1929 than any other major-league team in the 20th century.

A century later, the name Tris Speaker remains significant in the annals of baseball history, and the story of Babe Ruth's hall-of-fame career will always start with his six seasons in a Red Sox uniform.

DENTON T. (CY) YOUNG
CLEVELAND (N) 1890-98
ST. LOUIS (N) 1899-1900
BOSTON (A) 1901-08
CLEVELAND (A) 1909-11
BOSTON (N) 1911
ONLY PITCHER IN FIRST HUNDRED
YEARS OF BASEBALL TO WIN 500 GAMES.
AMONG HIS 511 VICTORIES WERE 3
NO-HIT SHUTOUTS. PITCHED PERFECT
GAME MAY 5, 1904. NO OPPOSING
BATSMAN REACHING FIRST BASE.

Denton True "Cy" Young is a name that has become synonymous with great pitching. The body of work he amassed over the course of his tremendous 22-season career is truly remarkable. His nickname, short for "Cyclone," was given to him because of his fastball. Hall-of-famer Honus Wagner said that Young had the greatest fastball he ever saw. Young is pictured below in his Boston uniform from 1903, a landmark season for both him and his team. He led the American League in wins, winning percentage, complete games, shutouts, saves, and innings pitched, and helped lead the team to its first world championship, defeating Pittsburgh five games to three. His record of 511 career pitching wins seems as safe as any baseball record that exists. He was elected in 1937. (Left, courtesy of Danny O'Brien.)

The great Cy Young displays the pitching form that allowed him to dominate the major leagues for two decades. More than a century after he played for the Red Sox, he still holds the team records for wins (192), complete games (275), and shutouts (38). Upon his passing in 1955, baseball created the Cy Young Award to honor the best pitchers each season. Red Sox pitchers have won the award seven times.

While all the attention is normally focused on his historic pitching, Young was also a reasonably good hitter. In this rare newspaper photograph, Cy Young is seen holding a bat in 1908. In the world championship season of 1903, he batted .321 in the regular season, and in game five of the World Series, he had three runs batted in, helping to secure his own victory.

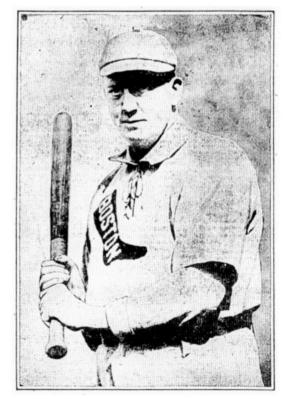

On August 13, 1908, Cy Young Day was held in Boston to honor the legendary pitcher. He was presented with many gifts and tokens of appreciation, including this impressive loving cup trophy from the *Boston Post* newspaper. Young is wearing the unique 1908 jersey, worn by the Red Sox only for that one season. Although 41 years old, he pitched his third no-hitter on June 30, 1908, against the New York Highlanders.

A statue honoring Cy Young was unveiled on the campus of Northeastern University on October 1, 1993, the 90th anniversary of game one of the first World Series won by Boston. It was erected near the site of the pitcher's mound of the old Huntington Avenue Grounds, the Red Sox ballpark for 11 seasons until Fenway Park officially opened in 1912, five days after the sinking of the *Titanic*.

THE GALLERY OF BOSTON STARS GROWS

The signing of established star Jimmy Collins by the brand-new American League Boston team in 1901 turned out to be a major coup. He became the most important figure in the team's first six seasons, managing from 1901 to 1906 as well as being the premier third baseman in the league. The world championship he led Boston to in 1903 helped put the league on equal footing with the long-established National League. Collins, the first third baseman enshrined, is ranked second in major-league history for putouts at the position, trailing only Brooks Robinson despite playing almost 1,200 fewer games at third base. Collins was elected in 1945.

JAMES COLLINS
CONSIDERED BY MANY THE GAME'S GREATEST THIRD BASEMAN, HE REVOLUTIONIZED STYLE OF PLAY AT THAT BAG. LED BOSTON RED SOX TO FIRST WORLD CHAMPIONSHIP IN 1903. A CONSISTENT BATTER, HIS DEFENSIVE PLAY THRILLED FANS OF BOTH MAJOR LEAGUES.

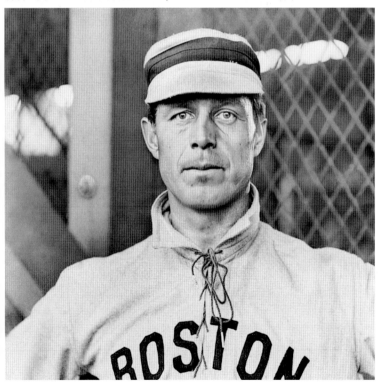

Collins is seen here in a formal portrait wearing his 1902 Boston Americans uniform. Aside from being a defensive wizard at third base, he was also a very fine hitter. He ranked among the American League leaders in numerous batting categories in his first several years in Boston. The speedy Collins recorded the first inside-the-park home run in team history in 1902.

In this inaugural franchise team photograph from 1901, manager/third baseman Jimmy Collins (first row, center) is directly in front of Cy Young. The Boston American League team had a hall of fame presence right from its inception. It would begin play in the Huntington Avenue Grounds ballpark constructed especially for the team just prior to the start of its maiden season. Collins recorded the first hit and first run in franchise history.

THE GALLERY OF BOSTON STARS GROWS

Jesse Burkett was one of the premier hitters in the National League in the 1890s and was a teammate of Cy Young for 10 seasons. He joined Young in Boston for the 1905 season, and while his hitting ability had declined, he managed to rank fourth in the American League in triples. Burkett had eight three-hit games for Boston, including one on the final day of the 1905 season, which turned out to be his last major-league game. He retired with a .339 batting average, and his 2,850 hits were second most at that time. Burkett lived most of his life in Worcester, Massachusetts, where he owned and managed a minor-league team and coached baseball at the College of the Holy Cross from 1917 to 1920. The Jesse Burkett Little League still operates there. He was elected in 1946.

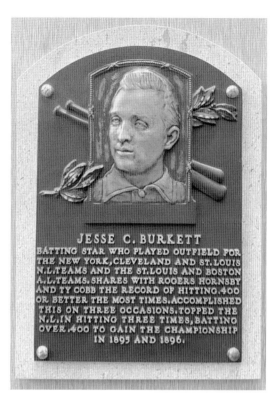

TRISTRAM E. (TRIS) SPEAKER
BOSTON (A) 1909 - 15
CLEVELAND (A) 1916 - 26
WASHINGTON (A) 1927
PHILADELPHIA (A) 1928
GREATEST CENTREFIELDER OF HIS
DAY. LIFETIME MAJOR LEAGUE BATTING
AVERAGE OF .344. MANAGER IN 1920
WHEN CLEVELAND WON ITS FIRST
PENNANT AND WORLD CHAMPIONSHIP.

Tristram Speaker was born in 1888 in Hubbard, Texas, a railroad town 70 miles from Dallas. Speaker became the full-time center fielder in 1909 and credited Cy Young for hitting him fly balls to help improve his outfield play. He went on to develop extraordinarily high skills in every phase of the game. With his truly elite performances at bat, on the basepaths, and in center field, he is regarded by some as the greatest all-around player to ever wear a Red Sox uniform. In 1912, Speaker had a 30-game hitting streak and won the American League Most Valuable Player, the franchise's first. The "Gray Eagle" played key roles in Boston's world championships of 1912 and 1915. He was elected in 1937.

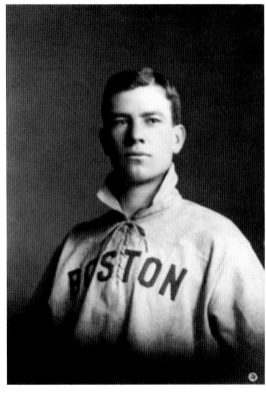

THE GALLERY OF BOSTON STARS GROWS

Seen here at Fenway Park around 1912, Tris Speaker works on his craft. He ranks among the most productive hitters of the 20th century. Speaker compiled a .345 lifetime batting average and 3,514 hits, both fifth in major-league history. His record of 792 doubles still stands and may never be equaled. Upon his retirement, only Ty Cobb had accumulated more hits.

Tris Speaker warms up his arm at Hilltop Park in New York before a game. Regarded as an all-around great player, he was an outstanding defensive center fielder, earning praise for his speed, range, and arm. His defensive prowess allowed him to accumulate the all-time records for career assists, career double plays, and single-season assists. Speaker also ranks second in career putouts behind fellow hall-of-famer Willie Mays.

HARRY BARTHOLOMEW HOOPER
BOSTON A.L. 1909-1920
CHICAGO A.L. 1921-1925
LEADOFF HITTER AND RIGHT FIELDER OF
1912-15-16-18 WORLD CHAMPION RED SOX.
NOTED FOR SPEED AND STRONG ARM.
COLLECTED 2,466 HITS FOR .281 CAREER
AVERAGE. HAD 3,981 PUTOUTS AND 344
ASSISTS. LIFETIME FIELDING AVERAGE .966.

Early in the 20th century, Harry Hooper was regarded as one of the finest defensive outfielders in the game in addition to being one of its best leadoff hitters. He patrolled right field for the Red Sox from 1909 to 1920. Hooper remains the only player in the team's history to contribute to four world championships, which he did in 1912, 1915, 1916, and 1918. In the 1915 World Series versus Philadelphia, he batted .350 and hit two home runs, including the game-five winner to clinch the series for Boston. It was Hooper who suggested to manager Ed Barrow in 1918 that young Babe Ruth be switched from pitcher to outfielder. Hooper was elected in 1971.

THE GALLERY OF BOSTON STARS GROWS

On display in a glass case at the Baseball Hall of Fame is Harry Hooper's c. 1916 Red Sox home uniform ball cap. Boston wore this plain white pinstriped style at home from 1912 to 1920. The Red Sox were the last major-league team in the 20th century to include a letter or logo on the front of their cap, adding a single red sock in 1931.

Harry Hooper (left) is pictured with Tris Speaker (center) and Duffy Lewis. The trio formed the Red Sox starting outfield from 1910 to 1915 and is regarded as one of the greatest of all time. The "Golden" or "Million-Dollar Outfield," as they were called, played a major role in Red Sox world championships in 1912 and 1915. Both Ty Cobb and Babe Ruth agreed this was the best outfield they had ever seen.

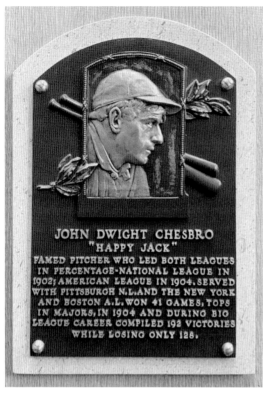

JOHN DWIGHT CHESBRO
"HAPPY JACK"
FAMED PITCHER WHO LED BOTH LEAGUES
IN PERCENTAGE-NATIONAL LEAGUE IN
1902; AMERICAN LEAGUE IN 1904. SERVED
WITH PITTSBURGH N.L. AND THE NEW YORK
AND BOSTON A.L. WON 41 GAMES, TOPS
IN MAJORS, IN 1904 AND DURING BIG
LEAGUE CAREER COMPILED 192 VICTORIES
WHILE LOSING ONLY 128.

Lifelong Massachusetts resident Jack Chesbro joined the hometown Red Sox for his final major-league stop in 1909. He had claimed his place in history in 1904 by earning 41 pitching wins, still an American League record. "Happy Jack" joined a Red Sox team that included Tris Speaker, Harry Hooper, and Smoky Joe Wood. His final start came on the last day of the season against his old New York Highlanders team. After retiring, Chesbro continued to pitch for many years with semipro teams in Western Massachusetts. As a young player in 1896, Chesbro bounced around with several semipro teams and even played for a stint in Cooperstown. Fifty years later, he found a permanent spot in Cooperstown with his enshrinement into the Baseball Hall of Fame in 1946.

THE GALLERY OF BOSTON STARS GROWS

GEORGE HERMAN (BABE) RUTH
BOSTON—NEW YORK, A.L.; BOSTON, N.L.
1914—1935
GREATEST DRAWING CARD IN HISTORY OF
BASEBALL. HOLDER OF MANY HOME RUN
AND OTHER BATTING RECORDS. GATHERED
714 HOME RUNS IN ADDITION TO FIFTEEN
IN WORLD SERIES.

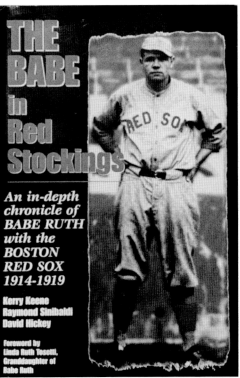

THE BABE in Red Stockings

An in-depth chronicle of BABE RUTH with the BOSTON RED SOX 1914-1919

Kerry Keene
Raymond Sinibaldi
David Hickey

Foreword by
Linda Ruth Tosetti,
Granddaughter of
Babe Ruth

The life of George Herman Ruth is a true American success story. Well into the 21st century, it is difficult to imagine a time when his name was not synonymous with baseball greatness. He developed a talent and passion for baseball at a boys' industrial school in Baltimore, and the legend began when the Boston Red Sox acquired him from the minor-league Baltimore Orioles in 1914. Ruth combined the ability to pitch with tremendous hitting that has not come close to being equaled in the entire history of baseball. In his first six seasons with Boston, Ruth was both one of the league's best pitchers and its most powerful slugger. By 1919, he was the most popular player in baseball, and to this day, he remains an American icon, a household name, and loved by Red Sox Nation. At left is the cover of *The Babe in Red Stockings*, which was released in 1997 and details in great depth, including game accounts, his entire career with the Boston Red Sox. Ruth was elected in 1936.

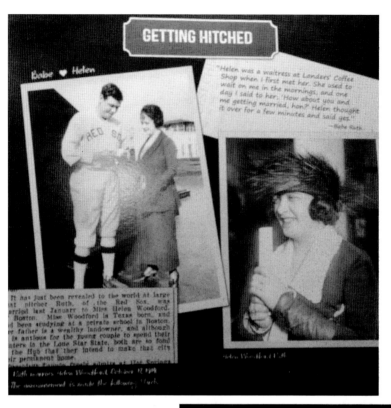

GETTING HITCHED

Babe ♥ Helen

"Helen was a waitress at Landers' Coffee Shop when I first met her. She used to wait on me in the mornings, and one day I said to her, 'How about you and me getting married, hon?' Helen thought it over for a few minutes and said yes."

—Babe Ruth

It has just been revealed to the world at large that pitcher Ruth, of the Red Sox, was married last January to Miss Helen Woodford, Boston. Miss Woodford is Texas born, and had been studying at a private school in Boston. Her father is a wealthy landowner, and although he is anxious for the young couple to spend their winters in the Lone Star State, both are so fond of the Hub that they intend to make this city their permanent home.

Ruth marries Helen Woodford October 17 1914
The announcement is made the following March

Helen Woodford Ruth

Ten days after the conclusion of the 1914 season, Babe Ruth married young Helen Woodford of Boston. After being acquired by Boston in July 1914, he began frequenting Lander's coffee shop, where Helen was a waitress. The celebration is shown here in a display at the hall of fame.

Young Ruth is pictured here during his first spring training with the Red Sox in Hot Springs, Arkansas, in 1915. Though still a full-time pitcher, Babe hit for a .315 batting average that season. Manager Bill Carrigan had enough confidence in Ruth's hitting ability that he sent him up to pinch-hit 10 times.

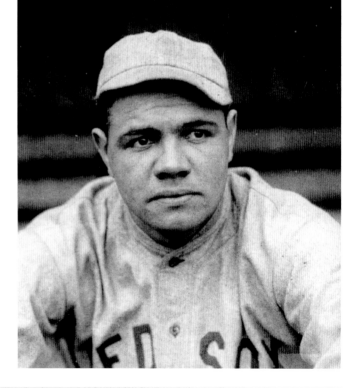

THE GALLERY OF BOSTON STARS GROWS

THE BOSTON RED SOX - AMERICAN LEAGUE CHAMPIONS - SEASON 1915

COLLINS P | WOOD P | GAINOR 1st B. | SHORE P | GREGG P | RUTH P | MAYS P | HOBLITZELL 1st B. | BARRY 2nd B. | GREEN TRAINER

LEONARD, P | HENRIKSEN U | GARDNER 3rd B | CARRIGAN MGR & C | CADY C | JANVRIN U | THOMAS C

LEWIS L.F. | WAGNER CAP & S.S. | SPEAKER C.F. | HOOPER R.F. | FOSTER P | SCOTT S.S.

Babe Ruth (third row center) is pictured with the 1915 world champion Red Sox. In his first full season, the 20-year-old earned a spot in the pitching rotation, compiling an impressive 18-8 record. Ruth threw a five-hit shutout against Washington in July at Fenway Park and showed a preview of his slugging ability by leading the team in home runs with four in 92 at bats. The Babe in red stockings had truly arrived. (Courtesy of John Hooper.)

BABE RUTH
P.—Boston Red Sox
151

A baseball card produced by the *Sporting News* in 1916 is one of the few depicting him in a Red Sox uniform. That season, at 21 years old, he blossomed into a star pitcher, winning 23 games, and led the American League in several categories. Babe remarkably allowed zero home runs in 323 innings pitched. Ruth likely would have won the Cy Young Award had it existed.

RED SOX IN THE HALL OF FAME

Holding his 42-ounce bat, Ruth is pictured at the 1918 World Series in Chicago. This was the first season he played multiple positions, often playing left field and first base on nonpitching days. Babe led the league in home runs along with winning 13 games. In game four of the World Series, he established a series record of 29 2/3 consecutive scoreless innings pitched, which stood for 43 years.

Displaying one of his lesser-known talents, a pipe-smoking Babe is tickling the ivories in his Sudbury, Massachusetts, home as wife Helen looks on. Legend has it that during a wintertime party there, a playful Babe pushed a piano out onto the ice of the nearby pond but was unable to push it back up the hill. It remained there, sinking to the bottom when the ice melted.

THE GALLERY OF BOSTON STARS GROWS

Babe Ruth Day was celebrated on September 20, 1919, between games of a doubleheader against Shoeless Joe Jackson and the White Sox. Ruth was presented with gifts of appreciation for his historic season. He hit his 27th home run to tie the major-league record in game one and would finish the season with 29. Game two would be his final game at Fenway Park with the Red Sox. (Courtesy of NBL.)

Although the 1919 Red Sox season concluded on September 28, Ruth appeared in several exhibition games over the following few weeks. On October 17 at Athletic Park in Scranton, Pennsylvania, he played in a charity game and is pictured here with members of the American Jewish Relief Committee. This is one of the last photographs of Ruth in a Red Sox uniform; he was traded to the Yankees a few months later.

HERBERT J. (HERB) PENNOCK
OUTSTANDING LEFT HANDED PITCHER IN
THE A.L. AND EXECUTIVE OF PHILADELPHIA
N.L. CLUB. AMONG RARE FEW WHO MADE
JUMP FROM PREP SCHOOL TO MAJORS. SAW
22 YEARS SERVICE WITH PHILADELPHIA,
BOSTON AND NEW YORK TEAMS IN A.L.
RECORDED 240 VICTORIES, 161 DEFEATS.
NEVER LOST A WORLD SERIES GAME,
WINNING FIVE. IN 1927, PITCHED 7⅓
INNINGS WITHOUT ALLOWING HIT IN
THIRD GAME OF SERIES.

"The Knight of Kennett Square" (Pennsylvania), left-handed pitcher Herb Pennock was acquired from the Philadelphia Athletics in June 1915, joining a team with a young Babe Ruth and star outfielders Tris Speaker and Harry Hooper. The first time he faced Ruth after Babe's sale to the Yankees, he held him hitless in four at bats. In the 1919 and 1920 seasons, Pennock was 23-8 at Fenway. He was elected in 1948.

Pennock is pictured at Fenway Park with his nine-year-old son Joe during the 1934 season. The 40-year-old pitcher returned to Boston to finish his career. Although primarily a reliever, he recorded his last two major-league wins with the Red Sox. He hurled a complete-game 13-1 win over the defending American League champion Washington Senators on June 1 in the nation's capital for the last of his 241 career wins.

THE GALLERY OF BOSTON STARS GROWS

In 1934, his second stint with Boston, Pennock is seen here before his final career start with Cleveland manager and future hall-of-famer Walter Johnson. Pennock was part of seven world championship teams, including two with the Red Sox. His daughter Jane married Eddie Collins Jr., whose father, Red Sox general manager Eddie Collins, had signed Pennock.

While World War I was raging in Europe, Pennock (second from left) put baseball on hold in 1918 to join the Navy. Initially avoiding the Navy baseball team, he was convinced to pitch a game versus the Army team at Chelsea Stadium on July 4 in Portsmouth, England, with the king in attendance. Pennock beat Army 2-1 in 10 innings. He returned to the Red Sox in 1919, becoming their most effective starter.

EDWARD GRANT BARROW

CLUB EXECUTIVE, MANAGER, LEAGUE
PRESIDENT IN MINORS AND MAJORS FROM
1894 TO 1945, CONVERTED BABE RUTH FROM
PITCHER TO OUTFIELDER AS MANAGER BOSTON
A.L. IN 1918, DISCOVERED HONUS WAGNER
AND MANY OTHER GREAT STARS. WON WORLD
SERIES IN 1918, BUILT NEW YORK YANKEES INTO
OUTSTANDING ORGANIZATION IN BASEBALL
AS BUSINESS MANAGER FROM 1920 TO 1945,
WINNING 14 PENNANTS, 10 WORLD SERIES.

In early 1918, Red Sox owner Harry Frazee hired Ed Barrow as manager. Barrow had managed the Detroit Tigers years earlier and had just resigned after several years as president of the International League, a top-level minor-league circuit. Barrow's shrewd moves helped elevate the Red Sox to World Series winners in 1918, capturing their third world championship in four seasons. Though Barrow was officially the field manager, he utilized his considerable executive experience to also perform general manager duties. It was Barrow who converted Babe Ruth from a pitcher to an everyday player. Below, he is pictured (far left) at the Red Sox executive offices with owner Harry Frazee (seated, right), Babe Ruth, and newly acquired first baseman Stuffy McInnis before the 1918 season. Barrow was elected in 1953.

As a pitcher for a semipro team in Baltimore, 19-year-old Waite Hoyt was invited to pitch Red Sox batting practice before a game in Washington. Impressed by the effort, Ed Barrow signed the youngster, known as "Schoolboy," and he started his first game at Fenway on July 31, 1919. Hoyt made an auspicious debut, beating Detroit 2-1 in a 12-inning complete game, and held the great Ty Cobb to one hit. Babe Ruth played outfield in all of Hoyt's starts that season, which included a 12 1/3–inning complete game in which he gave up five hits and lost. Hoyt started out 1920 well but missed 10 weeks with an abdominal injury. He was elected in 1969.

HUGH DUFFY
BRILLIANT AS A DEFENSIVE OUTFIELDER
FOR THE BOSTON NATIONALS, HE
COMPILED A BATTING AVERAGE IN 1894
WHICH WAS NOT TO BE CHALLENGED
IN HIS LIFETIME • .438.

When the diminutive 86-year-old man in a Boston uniform was enthusiastically giving batting instruction to young players at their 1953 training camp, few of them were fully aware of his history. Hugh Duffy had been one of the greatest hitters in the National League in the 1890s, and his .440 batting average in 1894 is the best in league history. He concluded his great playing career in 1906, and 15 years later, was hired to manage the Red Sox. After his two-season tenure at the helm, Duffy held several other positions within the Sox organization over the following few decades, including coach, scout, and front office roles. He developed a friendship with a much younger Ted Williams, as the two enjoyed discussing hitting. Born in Rhode Island, Duffy lived most of his life in Boston. He was elected in 1945.

Fifteen years before donning a Red Sox uniform to manage the team, Frank Chance's legend was born. As the manager/first baseman of the Chicago Cubs, he led them to back-to-back world championships in 1907 and 1908. At that time, a famous poem repeated the line "Tinker to Evers to Chance," highlighting his team's double-play proficiency. Chance retired after the 1914 season and returned to his native California. In 1923, he was lured out of retirement by Red Sox owner Harry Frazee. Unfortunately, Frazee had traded or sold off most of the better players, and Chance, with very little to work with, was dismissed after the season. Below, Chance shakes hands with Yankees manager Miller Huggins. Chance was elected in 1946.

CHARLES HERBERT RUFFING
"RED"

BOSTON, A.L. 1924-1930
NEW YORK, A.L. 1930-1946
CHICAGO, A.L., 1947

WINNER OF 273 GAMES.
WON 20 OR MORE GAMES IN EACH OF FOUR
CONSECUTIVE SEASONS. LED IN COMPLETE
GAMES 1928. TIED IN SHUTOUTS 1938-1939.
WON 7 OUT OF 9 WORLD SERIES DECISIONS.
SELECTED FOR ALL STAR TEAMS
1937-1938-1939

Acquired by the Red Sox in late 1923, pitcher Charles "Red" Ruffing made his major-league debut the following spring at the age of 19. In his third appearance, he held Babe Ruth hitless and struck him out once. The following season, he had complete-game shutouts in consecutive starts. Over his seven seasons with the team, dozens of his quality starts turned to losses or no-decisions due to lack of support both offensively and defensively. In 1928, Ruffing led the American League in complete games with 25. Also an outstanding hitter, he hit over .300 twice while with Boston. He was elected in 1967.

THE GALLERY OF BOSTON STARS GROWS

Yawkey's Way

Born in Detroit in 1903, Thomas Yawkey Austin lost both parents by the age of 15. Young Thomas was adopted by his uncle William Yawkey, a lumber and iron tycoon who owned the Detroit Tigers in the early 20th century. The renamed Thomas Austin Yawkey grew up mainly in New York City, and when his uncle passed away in 1918, he inherited an estimated $10 million, which was held in trust until his 30th birthday.

In the meantime, he graduated from Yale University in 1925 and went to work for the family business. Passionate about baseball, he became acquainted with Athletics star Eddie Collins, who like Yawkey was an alumnus of the Irving Prep School in Tarrytown, New York. While serving as a coach for the Athletics in the early 1930s, Collins helped facilitate Yawkey's purchase of the Red Sox from longtime owner Bob Quinn. In late February 1933, less than a week after he came into his full fortune, he paid $1.5 million for the Red Sox and Fenway Park. Both the team and the ballpark were badly in need of improvement, and so began his 44-season ownership of the Boston Red Sox.

Yawkey went on to be regarded as one of the more prominent executives in baseball during the mid-20th century. He also served as vice president of the American League from 1956 to 1973 and on the hall of fame's board of directors.

When Yawkey passed away in 1976, the Yawkey Foundation was created, and has continued its great work well into the 21st century. Ted Williams adored Tom Yawkey and described him as unselfish, fair, sincere, and honest. Williams once said, "he had a heart as big as a watermelon."

THOMAS AUSTIN YAWKEY

GAVE BASEBALL MORE THAN FOUR DECADES OF DEDICATED SERVICE AS OWNER-PRESIDENT OF BOSTON RED SOX FROM 1933 TO 1976. RATED ONE OF SPORT'S FINEST BENEFACTORS. SET PRECEDENT FOR A.L. IN 1936 AS FIRST TO HAVE TEAM TRAVEL BY PLANE. HIS CLUB WON PENNANTS IN 1946, 1967 AND 1975—AND NARROWLY MISSED IN 1948, 1949 AND 1972. VICE-PRESIDENT OF A.L. FROM 1956 TO 1973.

Upon purchasing the Red Sox at 30 years old in 1933, Tom Yawkey became the youngest major-league team owner. By his 44th season of ownership in 1976, he had become one of the game's elder statesmen. His ownership ended upon his death and was truly the end of an era for the Red Sox organization. He was the last American League owner left from 1933, and only Chicago Cubs owner Philip Wrigley remained in the National League. Yawkey and Wrigley were the only owners to have complete controlling interest in their teams throughout the entire period. Aside from his role as Red Sox owner and president, he also served on various executive baseball committees. When Yawkey was elected to the hall of fame by the Veterans Committee in 1980, four years after his passing, he became the first member inducted exclusively as an owner.

The new Red Sox owner dons the cap of his team in 1933. Yawkey was a fan of his team and his players and simply loved the game. He loved taking batting practice at Fenway Park and dreamed of hitting a ball over the left field "Green Monster," though he reportedly never succeeded. A world championship was his main goal, but the team fell one game shy in 1946, 1967, and 1975.

Tom Yawkey (center) is pictured with Eddie Collins (left) and newly hired manager Bucky Harris at a major-league meeting in New York in late 1933. Harris was the first field manager Yawkey hired, and Yawkey did so without consulting general manager Eddie Collins. Harris and Collins had feuded as opposing second basemen in the 1920s and did not have a smooth working relationship while in Boston. All three would later be elected to the hall of fame.

Yawkey chats with 20-year-old rookie Ted Williams in the Boston dugout before a game in 1939. The owner is sporting the baseball centennial patch on his shirt that was featured on all major-league uniforms that season. The two men had a close relationship right from the beginning that lasted until Yawkey's death from leukemia in 1976. Williams often fished with Yawkey on his wildlife preserve in South Carolina.

Yawkey and Ted Williams are all smiles in the owner's office at Fenway Park on February 4, 1956, as Williams signs his contract for the upcoming season. There was no doubt Yawkey was satisfied that the 38-year-old player earned his $50,000 salary that season. He had yet another all-star season with 24 home runs, led the majors in on-base percentage, and his .345 batting average was second only to Mickey Mantle.

Tom Yawkey's legacy has recently been tarnished because the Red Sox were the last major-league team to include a black player on their roster, when Elijah "Pumpsie" Green made his debut in 1959. In fact, Yawkey gave his general managers free rein in player acquisitions, and several black players were signed in the 1950s and spent time in the minor-league system. Biographer Bill Nowlin spent four years researching Yawkey and stated unequivocally that he could find no evidence that Yawkey held animus toward African Americans. Like Green, Reggie Smith (above) stated that Yawkey treated him well and even offered him money for a down payment on a house. Smith also defended Yawkey when Boston moved to change the name of the street near Fenway Park, called Yawkey Way. Below is Jim Rice with Yawkey.

In 1947, Dr. Sidney Farber helped create the Children's Cancer Research Foundation, which led to the establishment of the Jimmy Fund. Tom Yawkey took it on as the main Red Sox charity after the Boston Braves moved to Milwaukee in 1953. Pictured from left to right at the construction of a new wing are Dr. Farber, Ted Williams, Carl Yastrzemski, Yawkey, and team general manager Dick O'Connell.

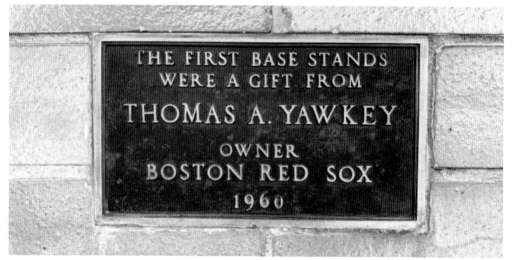

In 1960, Paul Kerr, president of the hall of fame, told a group of baseball executives that the dilapidated grandstands at Cooperstown's Doubleday Field would not pass another safety inspection. A short time later, Tom Yawkey, in his lifelong philanthropic spirit, intervened and donated the necessary resources to construct a new grandstand along the first base line. This plaque remains at the entrance of the grandstand to this day.

RED SOX PLAQUE
PARADE MARCHES ON

When Tom Yawkey bought the Red Sox and Fenway Park in 1933, it signaled a sorely needed change from the manner in which the franchise had operated for many years. The lack of financial resources that had plagued it for so long were now in the past. The new man in charge had deep pockets, desperately wanted a winner, and was willing to spend whatever it took to bring a championship to Boston.

Along with a complete renovation of Fenway Park, Yawkey instructed new general manager Eddie Collins to acquire star players to improve the team. Several of these established players, such as Lefty Grove, Joe Cronin, and Jimmie Foxx, helped change the team's image. They had all been winners and were building impressive future hall-of-fame credentials.

Toward the latter part of the 1930s, Collins focused more on developing young players in the minor leagues, such as Bobby Doerr, Ted Williams, and others. This approach finally paid dividends by 1946, and with a nucleus of home-grown players, an American League pennant would fly at Fenway for the first time in 28 years. Unfortunately, a world championship narrowly escaped Boston in a 4-3 loss to St. Louis in game seven of the World Series. Collins would go on to have a greater impact on the team than any man other than Yawkey himself.

Throughout these rebuilding years, more hall-of-fame players would pass through Boston and play for the Red Sox on their way to Cooperstown.

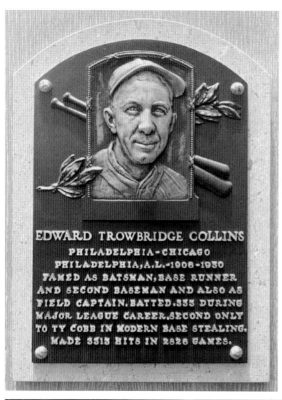

EDWARD TROWBRIDGE COLLINS
PHILADELPHIA - CHICAGO
PHILADELPHIA, A.L. -1906-1930
FAMED AS BATSMAN, BASE RUNNER
AND SECOND BASEMAN AND ALSO AS
FIELD CAPTAIN. BATTED .333 DURING
MAJOR LEAGUE CAREER, SECOND ONLY
TO TY COBB IN MODERN BASE STEALING.
MADE 3515 HITS IN 2826 GAMES.

One of Tom Yawkey's first acts when he took over the Red Sox in 1933 was finding someone within the game to run the team. He could not have found a better man with a higher baseball IQ than former superstar Eddie Collins. After receiving an Ivy League education at Columbia University, Collins had a 25-year career as one of the finest all-around second basemen of his era. A highly intelligent player with leadership qualities, he helped lead his teams to six World Series, winning four. Collins had been a player-manager with the White Sox in the mid-1920s and after retirement as a player served as a coach for the Athletics in 1931 and 1932. Collins assumed control of the Red Sox front office in 1933 and is pictured at left below with Tom and Elise Yawkey in the newly refurbished Fenway Park in 1934. Collins was elected in 1939.

RED SOX PLAQUE PARADE MARCHES ON

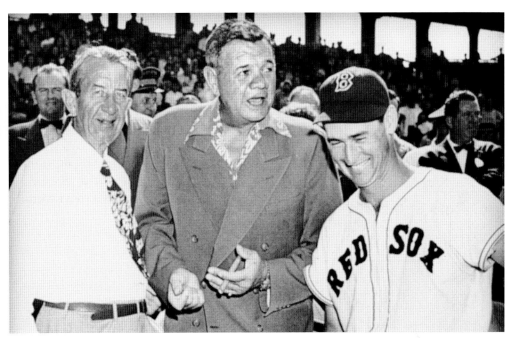

Boston general manager Eddie Collins hosts the great Babe Ruth on September 12, 1947. Unbeknownst at the time, this would be Ruth's final visit to Fenway Park. Ted Williams dropped by to renew acquaintances with the legendary slugger just prior to taking the field against the Cleveland Indians. Eleven months later, Ruth lost his long battle with cancer.

Collins has a pregame chat with Yankees pitcher Red Ruffing and Red Sox slugger Jimmie Foxx. All three men competed against each other at various junctures, most often when Ruffing was pitching for Boston in the 1920s. Foxx was elected to the hall of fame in 1951, the same year Collins passed away, and Ruffing was elected in 1967 and inducted three days after Jimmie's passing.

RED SOX IN THE HALL OF FAME

RICHARD BENJAMIN FERRELL
ST. LOUIS A.L. 1929-1933, 1941-1943
BOSTON A.L. 1933-1937
WASHINGTON A.L. 1937-1941, 1944-1947
CAUGHT MORE GAMES (1,806) THAN ANY OTHER
AMERICAN LEAGUER. DURABLE DEFENSIVE STAND-OUT
WITH FINE ARM. EXPERT AT HANDLING PITCHERS.
MET CHALLENGE OF 4 KNUCKLE-BALLERS IN SENATORS'
STARTING ROTATION. OFTEN FORMED BATTERY WITH
BROTHER, WES. HIT OVER .300 4 TIMES. SECOND
ONLY TO DICKEY IN A.L. CAREER PUTOUTS AT
RETIREMENT.

Considered one of the best catchers in the American League, Rick Ferrell was one of the first star players acquired by Tom Yawkey in 1933. When baseball's first All-Star Game was played later that season, American League manager Connie Mack used Ferrell for the entire game. He represented the Red Sox in the following three midsummer classics as well. From 1934 to 1937, he formed a pitcher/catcher combo in Boston with his brother Wes, an outstanding hurler. They were traded together to Washington in June 1937. Though Rick was technically elected to Cooperstown as a catcher, there is little doubt that in his case it was a lifetime achievement honor as well. Ferrell worked for four different teams in various capacities, including player, coach, scout, general manager, and vice president, for 63 years. He was elected in 1984.

Although a good hitting catcher, it was Rick Ferrell's defensive work behind the plate that really stood out. When his playing career ended in 1947, Ferrell had caught more games than any catcher in American League history, but it was the proficiency in those games that made him great. In the categories of putouts, assists, double plays, and runners caught stealing, he ranked in the top two among American League catchers 21 times.

Ferrell and brother Wes (left) were teammates in Boston from 1934 to 1937. Wes was traded from Cleveland to Boston one year after Rick had been acquired. On July 19, 1933, pitching for Cleveland against Boston at Fenway, Wes homered in the fourth inning. In the bottom half of the inning, Rick responded by homering off Wes, thus marking the first time in major-league history that brothers homered in the same game. (Courtesy of Richard Thompson.)

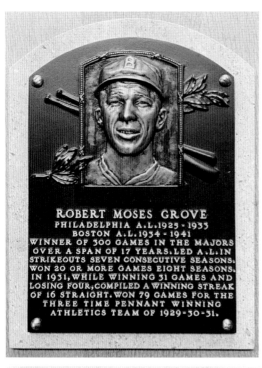

ROBERT MOSES GROVE
PHILADELPHIA A.L.1925 - 1933
BOSTON A.L.1934 - 1941
WINNER OF 300 GAMES IN THE MAJORS
OVER A SPAN OF 17 YEARS. LED A.L. IN
STRIKEOUTS SEVEN CONSECUTIVE SEASONS.
WON 20 OR MORE GAMES EIGHT SEASONS.
IN 1931, WHILE WINNING 31 GAMES AND
LOSING FOUR, COMPILED A WINNING STREAK
OF 16 STRAIGHT. WON 79 GAMES FOR THE
THREE TIME PENNANT WINNING
ATHLETICS TEAM OF 1929-30-31.

Tom Yawkey made his first truly eye-opening transaction to create a winning team on December 12, 1933. He paid the Philadelphia Athletics $125,000 for Lefty Grove, one of the premier pitchers in the American League since the mid-1920s. Grove had been a perennial league leader and key member of three pennant-winning teams. His first season with Boston in 1934 was injury-plagued and disappointing, but he bounced back in 1935 with 20 wins. He also led the league in earned run average, which he would do three more times in his eight years with Boston. Lefty was named to five All-Star teams in that span, and his final major-league victory in July 1941 was the 300th of his illustrious career. Between 1927 and 1960, Grove was the only pitcher to reach that milestone. He was elected in 1947.

TIMES, SATURDAY, JULY 26, 1941.

Games; Dodgers Lose Twice; Giants Triu

ET BACK
1, 8-4, 8-2

eak to Seven
Third Place
and Giants

TO FIFTH

Routed as
Blow to
rations

VETERAN WHO ENTERED PITCHING HALL OF FAME

Lefty Grove (center) being congratulated by his catcher, Johnny Peacock (left), and Jimmy Foxx, in the Red Sox clubhouse after he hung up his 300th triumph.

CUB ERRC
GIANTS

Four Unearne
Follow Dahl
on Doub

YOUNG, BA

Olsen Lasts
but French
—Lohrm

Dodgers' Box Scores

Grove Registers 300th Victory
A. Red Sox Check Indians, 10-6

Grove throws in foul territory before a game at the newly remodeled Fenway Park around 1934. Many questioned the wisdom of the enormous purchase price of Grove as his first season was dramatically affected by arm woes. After his subpar eight-win season, Lefty went home and learned to perfect his curve ball and subsequently added a fork ball. Grove returned to form and dominated for five more seasons.

Lefty Grove was known to be a frequent visitor to the Red Sox executive offices. Friendly with Tom Yawkey, he would occasionally be found in his office with his feet up on the owner's desk. Grove is seen here with general manager Eddie Collins in his office in 1940. The two had been with the Athletics from 1927 to 1932 and remained friendly throughout their years in Boston.

In an unusual scene, Grove is warming up before a game in 1937 as a marching band plays behind him. At 37 years old, he was in the midst of a great five-season stretch. A bit of bad luck plagued him this season. Even though he pitched complete games of 12 innings twice and 11 innings once, all were lost due to insufficient run support.

Nearly a century after his career began, Lefty Grove stands alone as the greatest left-handed pitcher in American League history. The achievements he amassed over a 17-season span are difficult to top. He led the league four times in wins while compiling 300 career victories. Grove led the league in earned run average eight times and strikeouts for seven consecutive years. He won 31 games, including 16 straight, in 1931.

RED SOX PLAQUE PARADE MARCHES ON

Grove is relaxing at home wearing his Red Sox warmup jacket, listening to his state-of-the-art Zenith console radio, and enjoying retirement. The radio was a gift from his Boston teammates in celebration of his 300th victory on July 25, 1941. Grove was also the proprietor of a pool hall and bowling alley called Lefty's Place in his hometown of Lonaconing, Maryland, which displayed much of his baseball memorabilia.

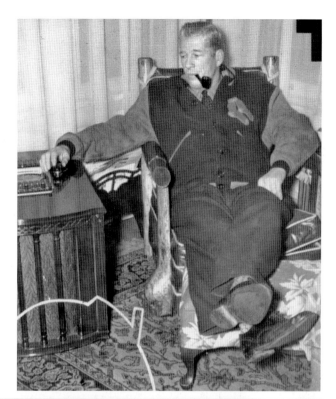

Hall-of-famer Lefty Grove returned to Fenway Park on May 19, 1958, and is seen here sitting in the dugout with old friend and teammate Ted Williams (right). The two had played together from 1939 to 1941. They were Grove's final three seasons and Williams's first three, and although Grove was 18 years older, they developed a mutual respect.

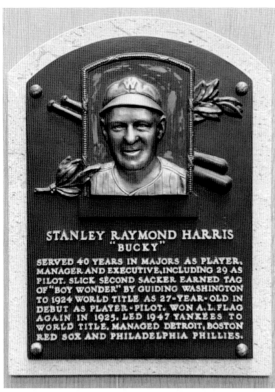

STANLEY RAYMOND HARRIS
"BUCKY"

SERVED 40 YEARS IN MAJORS AS PLAYER,
MANAGER AND EXECUTIVE, INCLUDING 29 AS
PILOT. SLICK SECOND SACKER EARNED TAG
OF "BOY WONDER" BY GUIDING WASHINGTON
TO 1924 WORLD TITLE AS 27-YEAR-OLD IN
DEBUT AS PLAYER-PILOT. WON A.L. FLAG
AGAIN IN 1925. LED 1947 YANKEES TO
WORLD TITLE. MANAGED DETROIT, BOSTON
RED SOX AND PHILADELPHIA PHILLIES.

After buying the Red Sox and acquiring several quality players, Yawkey hired proven winning manager Bucky Harris. He is seen below with Washington manager Joe Cronin as President Roosevelt throws out the first pitch at Griffith Stadium on opening day 1934. Although only 37 years old, Harris brought to the Sox 10 years of managing experience, back-to-back pennants, and a World Series title with Washington in 1924. Harris led the Sox to a modest fourth-place finish, although they improved by winning more games than they had since their world championship season of 1918. Harris managed four other teams over the course of his 29-year career, winning a total of 2,158 games, good for third on the all-time list when he retired in 1956. Harris died in 1977 on his 81st birthday. He was elected in 1975.

RED SOX PLAQUE PARADE MARCHES ON

By the age of 28, Joe Cronin had established himself as the finest shortstop in baseball, and he remains the youngest manager to take his team to the World Series. He had been named player-manager of Washington before the 1933 season at just 26 years old. Two years later, Tom Yawkey offered the Senators an unfathomable $250,000 amidst the Great Depression to have Cronin fill the same role on the Red Sox, which he did for 11 seasons. In his first season managing strictly from the bench, he took the 1946 Red Sox to the World Series, losing in seven games to St. Louis. Cronin represented Boston in the All-Star Game as a player five times and once as a manager. He also holds the rare major-league distinction of being a star player, manager, general manager, and league president. He was elected in 1956.

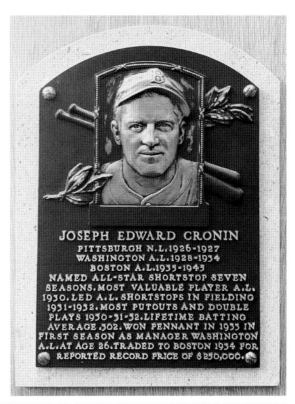

New Red Sox manager Cronin is pictured in the dugout at Fenway Park in April 1935 with Boston Braves outfielder Babe Ruth and manager Bill McKechnie. Babe returned to Boston after 15 seasons with the Yankees to conclude his playing career and participated in the annual exhibition game held between the Red Sox and Braves. McKechnie joined Cronin and Ruth in Cooperstown in 1962.

Cronin is pictured here with several of the most elite contemporary ballplayers of the 1930s. They are gathered at the 1937 All-Star Game at Griffith Stadium in Washington, DC, which was won by the American League 8-3. From left to right are Lou Gehrig, Cronin, Bill Dickey, Joe DiMaggio, Charlie Gehringer, Jimmie Foxx, and Hank Greenberg. Cronin and Greenberg would be inducted into the hall of fame the same year. (Courtesy of *Sporting News* archives.)

This button was handed out to fans entering Fenway Park on September 7, 1938, to celebrate Joe Cronin Day. The manger/shortstop was in his fourth year with the Red Sox and having one of his finest seasons, leading the team to its most wins in two decades. On this day, Cronin's double drove in the first run as the Red Sox beat Red Ruffing and the Yankees 11-5. (Courtesy of Henry Hickey.)

Cronin is pictured with Tom Yawkey at Ebbets Field for game two of the 1946 National League playoff between Brooklyn and St. Louis. Cronin was scouting the teams, as the winner would appear in the World Series against his Red Sox in three days. He ultimately convinced the American League to institute a one-game playoff for future ties rather than a best-of-three-games format.

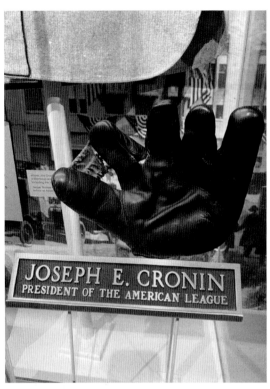

JOSEPH E. CRONIN
PRESIDENT OF THE AMERICAN LEAGUE

In addition to Cronin's plaque, the hall's museum section displays the early-20th-century-style glove he used at shortstop, where he played 1,843 games. Upon his retirement, he had participated in more double plays than any shortstop in American League history. Also featured is the name plate from the Boston office where Cronin served as American League president, becoming the first ex-player to hold the title.

The first two uniform numbers retired by the Boston Red Sox were No. 4 for Joe Cronin and No. 9 for Ted Williams. The ceremony was held before a Red Sox game on May 29, 1984, and Williams is shown here with Jean Yawkey seated to his left. Cronin, though ill at the time, was watching from a luxury box high up on the third base side.

Heinie Manush was one of the more underrated hitters of the 1920s and 1930s, compiling a .330 lifetime batting average. He was traded by the Washington Senators to the Red Sox in December 1935 at the age of 34, entering his 14th big-league season. Manush brought a bit more star power to a 1936 Boston team that already featured future hall-of-famers Jimmie Foxx, Lefty Grove, Joe Cronin, and Rick Ferrell. He was basically a part-time player, appearing in 72 games in left field and pinch-hitting on occasion. Manush had one seven-game stretch in late July in which he went 16 for 34 at the plate. He was elected in 1964.

HENRY EMMET MANUSH
1923 – 1939
SLUGGING OUTFIELDER
FOR 6 MAJOR LEAGUE CLUBS. BATTING
CHAMPION OF A.L. AT .378 WITH 1926 TIGERS.
LIFETIME AVERAGE OF .330 IN 2,009
MAJOR LEAGUE GAMES. HAD 2,524 HITS.

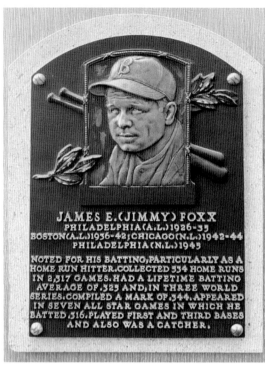

JAMES E. (JIMMY) FOXX
PHILADELPHIA (A.L.) 1926-35
BOSTON (A.L.) 1936-42; CHICAGO (N.L.) 1942-44
PHILADELPHIA (N.L.) 1945

NOTED FOR HIS BATTING, PARTICULARLY AS A
HOME RUN HITTER. COLLECTED 534 HOME RUNS
IN 2,317 GAMES. HAD A LIFETIME BATTING
AVERAGE OF .325 AND, IN THREE WORLD
SERIES, COMPILED A MARK OF .344. APPEARED
IN SEVEN ALL STAR GAMES IN WHICH HE
BATTED .316. PLAYED FIRST AND THIRD BASES
AND ALSO WAS A CATCHER.

In December 1935, Eddie Collins utilized Tom Yawkey's considerable financial resources to acquire slugging first baseman Jimmie Foxx. Only 28 at the time, Foxx had already won two MVP awards and a Triple Crown. Nicknamed "The Beast" due to his power and muscular physique, he was also called by some "the right-handed Babe Ruth." He was second only to Ruth in career home runs at the time with 303 and went on to hit his 400th and 500th homers with the Red Sox over the next six seasons. Foxx's 1938 season remains one of the greatest offensive performances in team history with 50 homers, 175 RBI, and a .349 batting average. "Double X" won his third MVP that season and came back strong with a second-place finish the following year. He was elected in 1951.

RED SOX PLAQUE PARADE MARCHES ON

Foxx and his new manager Joe Cronin are pictured on March 7, 1936, at the slugger's first Red Sox training camp in Sarasota, Florida. He joined Cronin, Lefty Grove, Rick Ferrell, and other recent acquisitions in Tom Yawkey's attempt to build a winning team. "The Beast" did not disappoint, as he played every game, batted .338, hit 41 home runs, had 143 runs batted in, and represented Boston in the All-Star Game.

Gathered at a nearly empty Fenway Park in the late 1930s are Jimmie Foxx (right), manager Joe Cronin (left), and general manager Eddie Collins. The three future hall-of-famers were among the most important additions that Tom Yawkey would make in his first few years of ownership. All three won Most Valuable Player awards during their stellar careers.

Although Foxx was primarily a first baseman, he showed versatility by also appearing in 142 games at third base, 109 games as catcher, 22 games in the outfield, and one game each at shortstop and pitcher. Foxx caught 42 games for the Red Sox in 1940 and is shown here in his only game behind the plate in 1937, with the Yankees' Lou Gehrig at bat.

Foxx is pictured with Dominic DiMaggio (left) and Ted Williams (right). The three appeared together in the Red Sox outfield for one game, with Ted in left, Dom in center, and Foxx in right. It was September 28, 1941, the final game of the season, against the Athletics in Philadelphia. History was made in this game, as Ted Williams went two for three to finish the season with his legendary .406 batting average. (Courtesy of Boston Public Library.)

RED SOX PLAQUE PARADE MARCHES ON

Leaning on the steps of the Boston dugout, Foxx is discussing a point with the umpire and looking very managerial in the process. After retiring as a player, he had a few stints as a minor-league manager in Portsmouth, Virginia; Bridgeport, Connecticut; and St. Petersburg, Florida. Perhaps his most interesting job as a manager came in 1952 with the Fort Wayne Daisies of the All-American Girls Professional Baseball League.

In a scene that became very common in Jimmie Foxx's time in Boston, he crosses home plate after hitting a home run. "The Beast" had a tremendously powerful swing custom made for Fenway Park. In his six-and-a-half seasons with the Red Sox, he hit 126 home runs at Fenway alone. In 1937, he achieved the very rare feat of hitting one completely over its center field wall.

ROBERT PERSHING DOERR

BOSTON, A.L., 1937 - 1951

QUIET LEADER OF RED SOX DURING 1940'S. CONSISTENT
SECOND BASEMAN, TOP DOUBLE PLAY MAN AND
FINE CLUTCH HITTER. LIFETIME BATTING AVERAGE
OF .288 WITH SIX SEASONS OF OVER 100 RBI'S. HELD
A.L. RECORD FOR 2B BY HANDLING 414 CONSECUTIVE
CHANCES WITHOUT ERROR. LED A.L. 2B IN DOUBLE
PLAYS FIVE TIMES, PUTOUTS FOUR TIMES AND ASSISTS
ON THREE OCCASIONS. BATTED .409 IN 1946 WORLD
SERIES.

Twenty-one-year-old rookie second baseman Bobby Doerr joined a Red Sox team in 1937 that featured Jimmie Foxx, Lefty Grove, and shortstop/manager Joe Cronin. He would become Cronin's double-play partner for the next several seasons, and years later, Cronin called Doerr "as fine a man as ever who wore a spiked shoe." Although he had several highly respected teammates such as Ted Williams, Dom DiMaggio, and Johnny Pesky, it was Doerr who was the captain of the team in the late 1940s. He became one of the most productive all-around second basemen of his time, with six 100-RBI seasons, and led his league in putouts, assists, or double plays at his position a total of 12 times. Sixteen years after retiring as a player, he served as the first base coach for the 1967 "Impossible Dream" Red Sox. He was elected in 1986.

Bobby Doerr, arguably the greatest second baseman in Red Sox history, was scouted along with Ted Williams by Eddie Collins in 1936. Pictured in action early in his career versus the White Sox at Comiskey Park around 1940, Doerr is doing one of the things he did best. He mastered the art of turning the double play and led the American League among second basemen five times.

One of the major tools of Bobby Doerr's trade, his baseball glove, is still on display in the hall of fame more than 70 years after his career concluded. Along with his impressive proficiency at the double play, he led the American League among second basemen in putouts four times and assists three times. If the Gold Glove award existed during Doerr's career, he likely would have won several.

Connecting for a hit at Fenway in 1939 is 21-year-old Bobby Doerr in his third season with the Red Sox. The emerging star infielder displays the swing that would produce 223 homers and 1,247 runs batted in, still all-time records for Red Sox second basemen. Doerr placed third in the Most Valuable Player voting in 1946 and batted .409 in Boston's trip to the World Series against St. Louis.

Six years after his retirement as a player, the Red Sox hired Doerr to be a roving minor-league instructor, a position he filled for 10 seasons. He is on hand at Fenway Park in 1961 to work with some of the younger players. Former teammate Ted Williams is present as well, helping rookie Carl Yastrzemski (8), who is waiting his turn in the batting cage.

The third uniform number retired by the Red Sox was Bobby Doerr's No. 1. Before a Fenway Park game on May 21, 1988, Ken Coleman (left), longtime broadcaster for the team, points to the right field facade, where a giant 1 is being revealed to the delight of the adoring crowd. In Doerr's rookie season of 1937, he wore No. 9, later made famous by Boston legend Ted Williams.

On hand for the unveiling of *The Teammates* statue outside of Fenway Park on June 9, 2010, are 91-year-old Doerr and 90-year-old Johnny Pesky. Based on the 2003 book by author/historian David Halberstam, it features the likenesses of the two former Red Sox infielders along with their lifelong friends Ted Williams and Dom DiMaggio.

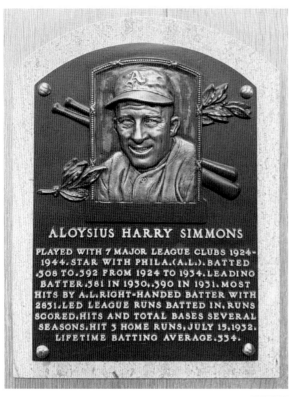

ALOYSIUS HARRY SIMMONS

PLAYED WITH 7 MAJOR LEAGUE CLUBS 1924-
1944. STAR WITH PHILA.(A.L.). BATTED
.308 TO .392 FROM 1924 TO 1934. LEADING
BATTER .381 IN 1930, .390 IN 1931. MOST
HITS BY A.L. RIGHT-HANDED BATTER WITH
2831. LED LEAGUE RUNS BATTED IN, RUNS
SCORED, HITS AND TOTAL BASES SEVERAL
SEASONS. HIT 3 HOME RUNS, JULY 15, 1932.
LIFETIME BATTING AVERAGE .334.

Al Simmons was one of the top superstars in baseball from the mid-1920s to the mid-1930s. He recorded batting averages above .350 six times, including .392 in 1927. Simmons started in baseball's first three All-Star Games from 1933 to 1935. After the 1941 season, he decided to stop playing and became a coach for the Philadelphia Athletics. Boston signed Simmons just before training camp in 1943 to help fill the void in left field with Ted Williams serving in the Navy. He was used sparingly but recorded his 2,900th hit at Fenway on April 29. Eighteen years before Carl Yastrzemski became the last Red Sox player to wear No. 8, Al donned it for this one season. He was elected in 1953.

RED SOX PLAQUE PARADE MARCHES ON

When Tom Yawkey promoted Joe Cronin (below, right) from manager to general manager after the 1947 season, there was no more experienced or qualified replacement than Joe McCarthy. In his 21 seasons managing the Cubs and Yankees, he had won over 1,900 regular-season games and seven World Series titles. He had resigned from the Yankees during the 1945 season due to health issues, but when Cronin called, McCarthy was ready to return. He improved the team by 13 wins in his first season, finishing in a first-place tie in the American League with Cleveland. Unfortunately, the Sox lost a one-game playoff, missing a chance to play the Boston Braves in the 1948 World Series. He retired from his position in June 1950, again citing health issues. He was elected in 1957.

JOSEPH VINCENT McCARTHY
CHICAGO N.L. 1926 - 1930
NEW YORK A.L. 1931 - 1946
BOSTON A.L. 1948 - 1950
OUTSTANDING MANAGER WHO NEVER PLAYED
IN MAJOR LEAGUES. THE MAJOR LEAGUE
TEAMS MANAGED BY HIM DURING 24 YEARS
NEVER FINISHED OUT OF FIRST DIVISION.
WON PENNANTS CHICAGO N.L. 1929,
NEW YORK A.L. 1932 - 6 - 7 - 8 - 9 - 41 - 2 - 3.
WON SEVEN WORLD'S CHAMPIONSHIPS WITH
NEW YORK YANKEES - FOUR OF THEM
CONSECUTIVELY 1936 - 7 - 8 - 9.

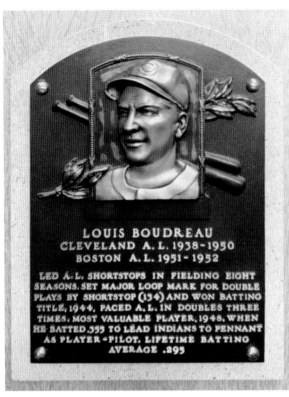

LOUIS BOUDREAU
CLEVELAND A. L. 1938-1950
BOSTON A. L. 1951-1952

LED A. L. SHORTSTOPS IN FIELDING EIGHT
SEASONS. SET MAJOR LOOP MARK FOR DOUBLE
PLAYS BY SHORTSTOP (134) AND WON BATTING
TITLE, 1944, PACED A. L. IN DOUBLES THREE
TIMES. MOST VALUABLE PLAYER, 1948, WHEN
HE BATTED .355 TO LEAD INDIANS TO PENNANT
AS PLAYER-PILOT. LIFETIME BATTING
AVERAGE .295

Lou Boudreau, who debuted with Cleveland in 1938, became one of the finest all-around shortstops in the game in the 1940s. He was so well respected that he became the Indians player-manager at 24 and remained in that dual role for nine seasons. Boudreau led his team to a World Series victory over the Boston Braves in 1948. Signing with the Red Sox in 1951, he joined a lineup with stars Ted Williams, Bobby Doerr, and Dom DiMaggio. Boudreau got off to a blazing start and hit in all but one of his first 15 games. Tom Yawkey hired Boudreau as player-manager for 1952, but he played himself only briefly that season and concentrated strictly on managing fulltime through 1954. Boudreau was elected in 1970.

RED SOX PLAQUE PARADE MARCHES ON

Manager Lou Boudreau (above, right) welcomes newly acquired George Kell to the Red Sox in 1952. Kell was the premier third baseman in the American League for over a decade in the 1940s and 1950s. Stellar on defense and an elite hitter, he hit in 16 of his first 17 games with Boston. Kell narrowly beat out Ted Williams for the 1949 American League batting title, denying Williams his third Triple Crown award. He wore uniform No. 1 while in Boston, a number previously worn by the great Bobby Doerr. Kell, a 10-time All-Star, and Ted Williams were the two Boston representatives on the 1953 squad. Kell was elected in 1983.

GEORGE CLYDE KELL
PHILADELPHIA A. L. 1943-1946
DETROIT A. L. 1946-1952
BOSTON A. L. 1952-1954
CHICAGO A. L. 1954-1956
BALTIMORE A. L. 1956-1957
PREMIER A. L. THIRD BASEMAN OF 1940'S AND
1950'S. SOLID HITTER AND SURE-HANDED FIELDER
WITH STRONG, ACCURATE ARM. BATTED OVER
.300 9 TIMES, LEADING LEAGUE WITH .343 IN
1949. LED A. L. THIRD BASEMEN IN FIELDING
PCT. 7 TIMES, ASSISTS 4 TIMES AND PUTOUTS
AND DOUBLE PLAYS TWICE.

It is unlikely that when Kell was fielding hard-hit balls at the "hot corner" he dreamed that the glove on his left hand would end up displayed in the hall of fame. Possessing terrific range and a strong throwing arm allowed him to rank near the top of several defensive categories. Kell owned the all-time career record for fielding percentage among third basemen until he was passed by Brooks Robinson.

George Kell (center) had three hits and three runs batted in to help Boston defeat the Yankees 10-9 on May 23, 1954. Immediately following the game, Kell was informed he had been traded to the Chicago White Sox. Dejected friend Ted Williams (left) looks on as Kell hands his uniform jersey to manager Lou Boudreau (right).

RED SOX PLAQUE PARADE MARCHES ON

THE KID IN BRONZE

It seems poetic that Ted Williams, affectionately known as "The Kid," "Teddy Ballgame," and the "Splendid Splinter," made his major-league debut in 1939, just weeks before the official opening of the Baseball Hall of Fame. It is almost as if Ted and the hall were made for each other. Twenty-seven years later, Williams would be inducted as one of baseball's all-time greats.

Ted Williams once said, "All I want out of life is that when I walk down the street folks will say, there goes the greatest hitter that ever lived." He would constantly talk about hitting, seeking advice from other great hitters and pitchers, and in 1970 wrote a book on the subject, *The Science of Hitting*. Not only is Ted at the top of that continuous debate, he accomplished many things other people can only dream about.

Most importantly, Williams helped raise tens of millions of dollars for cancer care and research through his lifelong association with the Jimmy Fund. He also served as an aviator in two wars, was inducted into the International Game Fish Association Hall of Fame, and received the Presidential Medal of Freedom from Pres. George H.W. Bush, the highest civilian award bestowed by the US government. He was also selected to Major League Baseball's All-Time and All-Century Teams in 1997 and 1999 respectively. After his retirement, he spent several summers teaching kids hitting and recalling baseball stories at the Ted Williams Baseball Camp in Lakeville, Massachusetts.

Williams won every imaginable award a player could win, but a World Series championship eluded him, having lost in his only appearance in 1946 to the Cardinals. To this day, he still holds the all-time major-league record for on-base percentage at .482.

More than 60 years after his retirement and almost a century after his major-league debut, Ted Williams is still regarded as one of the best hitters who ever lived, just as he imagined. The beloved Williams will live forever in the hearts and minds of Red Sox fans everywhere.

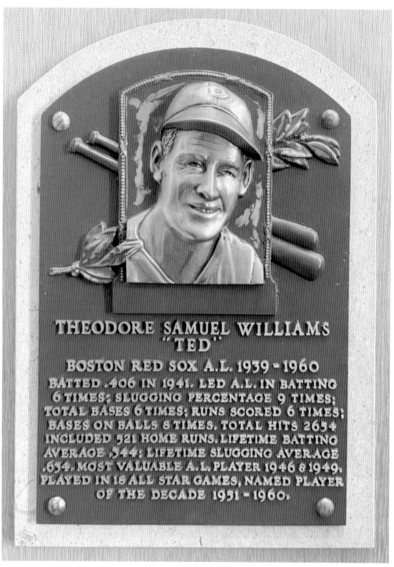

THEODORE SAMUEL WILLIAMS
"TED"
BOSTON RED SOX A.L. 1939 - 1960
BATTED .406 IN 1941. LED A.L. IN BATTING
6 TIMES; SLUGGING PERCENTAGE 9 TIMES;
TOTAL BASES 6 TIMES; RUNS SCORED 6 TIMES;
BASES ON BALLS 8 TIMES. TOTAL HITS 2654
INCLUDED 521 HOME RUNS. LIFETIME BATTING
AVERAGE .344; LIFETIME SLUGGING AVERAGE
.634. MOST VALUABLE A.L. PLAYER 1946 & 1949.
PLAYED IN 18 ALL STAR GAMES, NAMED PLAYER
OF THE DECADE 1951 - 1960.

In a century and a half of professional baseball, few have reached a stature within the game equal to Theodore Samuel Williams. Named after former US president Theodore Roosevelt, Williams became an extremely noteworthy figure not only in baseball but in the US military and as a fisherman as well. His historic major-league career, spanning parts of four decades, began when the great Lou Gehrig was still active, was interrupted by a call to war as an aviator in World War II and Korea, and ended in glorious fashion with a home run in his last career at bat. The 20-year-old "Kid" played like a hall-of-famer from the start and was subsequently named to 18 All-Star teams. Williams shares the distinction of capturing two batting Triple Crowns with only Rogers Hornsby, missing out on a third by the slimmest of margins. Many have speculated that without missing nearly five seasons due to military service, he may have approached 700 career home runs. Ted Williams, thought of by some as the real-life John Wayne, was the most important man to wear a Red Sox uniform. He was elected in 1966.

THE KID IN BRONZE

Though he had seemingly already attained immortal status, it was made official on July 25, 1966, with Ted's induction into the Baseball Hall of Fame. That day, he was joined by former Yankees manager Casey Stengel as the new members of baseball's hallowed shrine. Williams is pictured here with his original bronze plaque, which he was not happy with because he felt it made him look older. He requested that they produce a new one with a different image, which they did shortly thereafter. When Ted gave his speech at the ceremony, he expressed the belief that the hall should elect former Negro League greats such as Satchel Paige and Josh Gibson. Within six years, both were elected, and the hall of fame was forever changed. Williams later served as a voting member of the hall's Veterans Committee from 1986 to 1996.

THEODORE SAMUEL WILLIAMS
"TED"
BOSTON RED SOX A.L. 1939-1960
BATTED .406 IN 1941. LED A.L. IN BATTING
6 TIMES; SLUGGING PERCENTAGE 9 TIMES;
TOTAL BASES 6 TIMES; RUNS SCORED 6 TIMES;
BASES ON BALLS 8 TIMES. TOTAL HITS 2654
INCLUDED 521 HOME RUNS. LIFETIME BATTING
AVERAGE 344. LIFETIME SLUGGING AVERAGE
634. MOST VALUABLE A.L. PLAYER 1946 & 1949.
PLAYED IN 18 ALL STAR GAMES. NAMED PLAYER
OF THE DECADE 1951 - 1960.

A young Ted Williams kneels in the on-deck circle at Fenway Park during his rookie season, intensely studying the pitcher he is about to face. Always striving for perfection, Williams would accept nothing less than being the best hitter he could be, and most observers saw a bright future for him. No one could have imagined the heights he reached over the following 21 years.

Rookie Ted Williams in 1939 imagined a career that would ultimately match his wildest dreams. Playing his first game in Yankee Stadium with Lou Gehrig at first base, he hit a double off hall-of-fame pitcher Red Ruffing. Three days later, he had his first four-hit game, and on August 29, the day before his 21st birthday, he hit a grand slam and drove in five runs.

THE KID IN BRONZE

In an unusual scene from his second season, Williams made his only career pitching appearance. It was August 24, 1940, at Fenway with Boston losing 11-1 to the eventual pennant-winning Detroit Tigers. Ted entered the game in the eighth inning and in two relief innings gave up just one run and struck out future teammate Rudy York, who had previously hit a home run in the game.

While the Red Sox were making their way north from Florida after spring training in 1941, young Ted Williams stopped by the Hillerich & Bradsby factory in Louisville, Kentucky. Williams was known to be extremely particular about his bats and would send a shipment back if he did not think they were perfect. He is seen here checking out a pile of Louisville Sluggers made to his specifications.

RED SOX IN THE HALL OF FAME

Seventy-five-year-old Red Sox coach Hugh Duffy is joking with young Ted Williams about the batting average he would need to reach for the single-season record. Duffy's .438 average with Boston's National League team in 1894 was long regarded as the record. Williams's final average in 1941 was .406 and is still considered a legendary feat. No one has hit .400 since, some 80 years later.

While "the greatest hitter of all-time" is still debated, Ted Williams's all-time career record of .482 on-base percentage indicates he was the most effective batsman. His scientific approach to hitting and strategy of looking for a good pitch were aided by superior eyesight. Seen here in his final season displaying his patented slightly upper-cut swing, he ended his career with 521 home runs and a lofty .344 batting average.

THE KID IN BRONZE

Aviator Williams is pictured below receiving one of the numerous medals he was awarded for his distinguished military service during both World War II and the Korean War. He initially joined the Navy Reserves in May 1942 and was activated early the following year. Williams was commissioned as a second lieutenant in the Marine Corps in May 1944. He trained to become a fighter pilot and subsequently became an instructor. Promoted to captain in the Marines, Williams was later recalled and saw combat action in Korea in 1952. On his first battle mission in February 1953, his Panther jet was shot down, forcing him to perform a crash landing, and Ted walked away with only a sprained ankle. He resumed flying the next day and was part of 38 more missions alongside future astronaut John Glenn, who was a fellow squadron member.

Three-year-old Ted poses with his mother May and younger brother Danny in their home city of San Diego in 1921. May, whose maiden name was Venzor, was born in El Paso, Texas, and was of Mexican descent. Her brother Saul, an accomplished amateur ballplayer, taught young Ted the game. Williams expressed the belief in later years that if his last name was Venzor and his Mexican heritage was widely known, he may well have faced a level of discrimination. Ted always showed empathy and compassion to those who experienced such indignities and was vocal about his displeasure at the time. Williams is pictured below with Elijah "Pumpsie" Green, who in 1959 became the first black player for the Red Sox. Though 15 years his senior, Ted served as his throwing warmup partner before games and also gave him batting tips.

THE KID IN BRONZE

Aside from hitting a baseball, one of Ted's biggest passions and talents was as an expert fisherman. Here, Williams displays the 1,235-pound marlin he caught on December 10, 1954, one of his prized catches. He traveled all over to fish, from the Florida Keys to New Brunswick, Canada, to New Zealand and Mozambique. Williams had a stint hosting a television show on fishing and made guest appearances on *Wide World of Sports* and *American Sportsman*. Below is a sculpture by Armand Lamontagne of Ted as a fisherman completed in 1997. It is on display at the Sports Museum of New England in Boston.

Tom Yawkey and the Red Sox stepped in and made the Jimmy Fund their main charity in 1953, filling the void created after the National League Boston Braves moved to Milwaukee. Ted Williams is signing autographs for children being treated at the Children's Cancer Research Foundation in Boston, later renamed the Dana-Farber Cancer Institute. Williams would continue to contribute his time and effort to the charity for the remainder of his life.

Two years after his passing, Williams was honored for all his work with the Jimmy Fund. On April 16, 2004, this impressive statue of Ted in his Red Sox uniform placing his cap on a small boy with cancer was unveiled outside Fenway Park's Gate B at Ipswich and Van Ness Streets. Former teammates Bobby Doerr and Johnny Pesky were on hand at the ceremony. (Courtesy of Josh Sinibaldi.)

THE KID IN BRONZE

It is difficult to imagine a greater collection of four active ballplayers together in one spot at the same time. The star-studded quartet of future hall-of-famers are considered among the greatest to have ever played the game. From left to right are Hank Aaron, Ted Williams, Stan Musial, and Willie Mays at the 1959 All-Star Game at the Los Angeles Memorial Coliseum. The four sluggers hit a combined 2,411 home runs over the course of their careers. Below, 40 years later, 80-year-old Williams makes a special appearance at the 1999 All-Star Game at Fenway Park in a pregame ceremony. Sitting at center in a white cap, Williams is surrounded by that era's great players, including Cal Ripken, Ken Griffey Jr., and Tony Gwynn. Aaron, Musial, and Mays were also on hand that night as the All-20th-Century Team was announced.

RED SOX IN THE HALL OF FAME

When Tom Yawkey's widow, Jean, saw sculptor Armand Lamontagne's recently completed statue of Babe Ruth in 1984, she commissioned the Rhode Island artist to create a similar work of Ted Williams. Starting with a 2,000-pound block of basswood, Lamontagne went to work, and when the statue was unveiled at the Baseball Hall of Fame on July 26, 1985, it brought tears to Williams's eyes. Upon Ted's death on July 5, 2002, the Red Sox held a memorial ceremony (below) billed as "Ted Williams: A Celebration of an American Hero" at Fenway Park. His No. 9 was emblazoned upon the left field turf, made up of 10,000 white carnations, as both present and former Boston players lined up in uniform in front of the left field wall. A soldier plays "Taps" on a bugle in the foreground. (Below, courtesy of Ray Sinibaldi.)

THE KID IN BRONZE

6

A New Cast of Legends

As Ted Williams was walking away from the game after the 1960 season at the age of 42, the torch was being passed to young Carl Yastrzemski and an emerging cast. Throughout the first half of the 1960s, there were noteworthy individual performances including batting titles, no-hitters, league leads, and a rookie of the year. Team success, however, continued to be elusive until the hiring of young manager Dick Williams after the 1966 season. Taking a strict, hardline approach, the rookie manager was able to take a cast of mainly young players and mold them into a Cinderella-like pennant winner. Though the so-called "Impossible Dream" came one victory short of becoming a reality, the die had been cast.

The revitalized franchise was now viewed as a potential winner by a whole new legion of fans. Finishing in the lower half of the league standings was no longer acceptable. The idea of going 21 years between postseason appearances was a thing of the past, as were crowds at Fenway of less than 5,000 people. Boston would make a return to the World Series in both the 1970s and 1980s, though to the chagrin of Red Sox fans, the deciding game seven would not go their way in either. The so-called "curse" would continue.

Throughout these years, however, the team introduced home-grown talent such as Carlton Fisk, Jim Rice, and Wade Boggs and brought aboard Cooperstown-bound stars Luis Aparicio, Tony Perez, and Tom Seaver, among others, to help the cause.

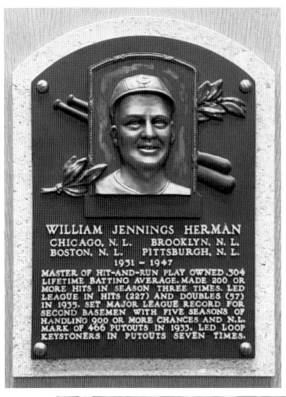

WILLIAM JENNINGS HERMAN
CHICAGO, N. L.   BROOKLYN, N. L.
BOSTON, N. L.   PITTSBURGH, N. L.
1931 – 1947
MASTER OF HIT-AND-RUN PLAY OWNED .304
LIFETIME BATTING AVERAGE. MADE 200 OR
MORE HITS IN SEASON THREE TIMES. LED
LEAGUE IN HITS (227) AND DOUBLES (57)
IN 1935. SET MAJOR LEAGUE RECORD FOR
SECOND BASEMEN WITH FIVE SEASONS OF
HANDLING 900 OR MORE CHANCES AND N.L.
MARK OF 466 PUTOUTS IN 1933. LED LOOP
KEYSTONERS IN PUTOUTS SEVEN TIMES.

Named to 10 consecutive National League All-Star teams, second baseman Billy Herman was unquestionably the premier player at his position from the mid-1930s to the mid-1940s. Herman spent more than a decade managing in the minor leagues. He returned to the majors as the Red Sox third base coach from 1960 to 1964 and assumed managerial responsibilities with two games remaining in the 1964 season. The Sox had fallen on tough times, as reflected in the fact that in Herman's final game as third base coach, the attendance at Fenway was a paltry 306 spectators. Herman remained on as manager until 1966 but was let go as he was unable to win with a nucleus of players who would become the 1967 "Impossible Dream" Red Sox. He was elected in 1975.

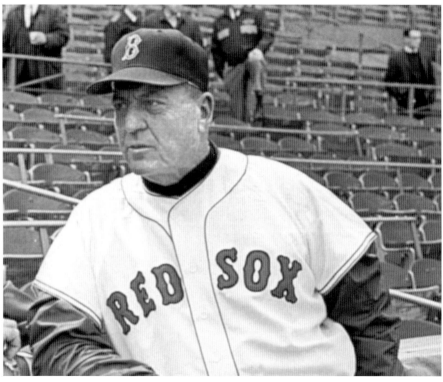

A NEW CAST OF LEGENDS

After the 1966 season, Red Sox general manager Dick O'Connell knew a bold move was needed to change the team's habit of finishing near the bottom of the league. He hired Dick Williams, the team's top minor-league manager, to change the "country club" culture. Upon his hiring, Williams went out on a limb, predicting "we'll win more than we lose." Many were skeptical, but the no-nonsense disciplinarian delivered well beyond expectations. The nucleus of the squad he took over was primarily under 25 years old, and he stressed the importance of fundamentals. Williams and his team shocked the baseball world, falling one win short of a world championship. For his efforts, he was honored with the Sporting News Manager of the Year Award. Although Williams had winning records with Boston the following two seasons, he was dismissed in September 1969. He was elected in 2008.

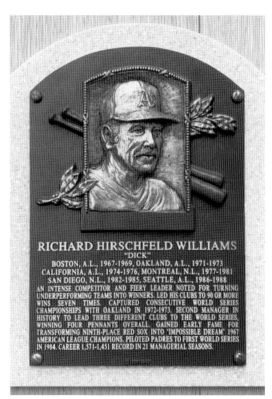

RICHARD HIRSCHFELD WILLIAMS
"DICK"
BOSTON, A.L., 1967-1969, OAKLAND, A.L., 1971-1973
CALIFORNIA, A.L., 1974-1976, MONTREAL, N.L., 1977-1981
SAN DIEGO, N.L., 1982-1985, SEATTLE, A.L., 1986-1988
AN INTENSE COMPETITOR AND FIERY LEADER NOTED FOR TURNING
UNDERPERFORMING TEAMS INTO WINNERS. LED HIS CLUBS TO 90 OR MORE
WINS SEVEN TIMES. CAPTURED CONSECUTIVE WORLD SERIES
CHAMPIONSHIPS WITH OAKLAND IN 1972-1973. SECOND MANAGER IN
HISTORY TO LEAD THREE DIFFERENT CLUBS TO THE WORLD SERIES,
WINNING FOUR PENNANTS OVERALL. GAINED EARLY FAME FOR
TRANSFORMING NINTH-PLACE RED SOX INTO 'IMPOSSIBLE DREAM' 1967
AMERICAN LEAGUE CHAMPIONS. PILOTED PADRES TO FIRST WORLD SERIES
IN 1984. CAREER 1,571-1,451 RECORD IN 21 MANAGERIAL SEASONS.

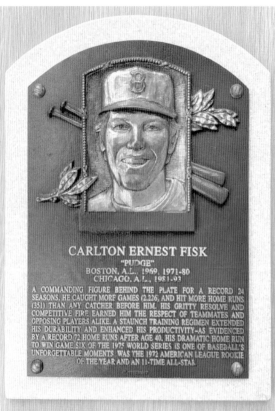

CARLTON ERNEST FISK
"PUDGE"
BOSTON, A.L., 1969, 1971-80
CHICAGO, A.L., 1981-93

A COMMANDING FIGURE BEHIND THE PLATE FOR A RECORD 24
SEASONS, HE CAUGHT MORE GAMES (2,226) AND HIT MORE HOME RUNS
(351) THAN ANY CATCHER BEFORE HIM. HIS GRITTY RESOLVE AND
COMPETITIVE FIRE EARNED HIM THE RESPECT OF TEAMMATES AND
OPPOSING PLAYERS ALIKE. A STAUNCH TRAINING REGIMEN EXTENDED
HIS DURABILITY AND ENHANCED HIS PRODUCTIVITY—AS EVIDENCED
BY A RECORD 72 HOME RUNS AFTER AGE 40. HIS DRAMATIC HOME RUN
TO WIN GAME SIX OF THE 1975 WORLD SERIES IS ONE OF BASEBALL'S
UNFORGETTABLE MOMENTS. WAS THE 1972 AMERICAN LEAGUE ROOKIE
OF THE YEAR AND AN 11-TIME ALL-STAR.

In April 1968, manager Dick Williams and his star players from the historic 1967 season pose with their respective awards earned on the way to winning the pennant. From left to right are Jim Lonborg (Cy Young Award), Williams (Sporting News Manager of the Year), Carl Yastrzemski (MVP, Triple Crown, Batting Champion, Gold Glove, Sporting News Player of the Year), and first baseman George "Boomer" Scott (Gold Glove). (Courtesy of Edward Dunham.)

Born in Bellows Falls, Vermont, and raised in Charleston, New Hampshire, Carlton Fisk has pure New England roo Playing for the Bellows Falls American Legion team in 1965, the 17-year-old hit home run in a tournament at Doubleda Field in Cooperstown, just steps away from the hall of fame. Fisk homered again on the same field in the 1975 Hal of Fame Game. He was elected in 2000.

A NEW CAST OF LEGENDS

Carlton Fisk was attending the University of New Hampshire on a basketball scholarship when he was drafted by the Red Sox in the 1967 amateur draft. He began his climb through Boston's minor-league system that summer, and after brief stints with the major-league squad in 1969 and 1971, he became the starting catcher in 1972. Fisk established himself in impressive fashion, running away with the American League Rookie of the Year Award and the Gold Glove award, placing fourth in Most Valuable Player voting, and being named to his first of 11 All-Star Games. In a rare feat for a catcher, he also led the league in triples. Fisk played until 1993, retiring at 45 years old.

RED SOX IN THE HALL OF FAME

Early in his second full season, Fisk received his American League Rookie of the Year Award for 1972, officially called the Ford C. Frick Award at that time. Bob Holbrook, an executive assistant for the American League, is presenting the award prior to a game versus the Yankees. Fisk was on his way to another All-Star selection and being regarded as one of the premier catchers in baseball.

Nearly half a century after it was hit, Fisk's game-winning home run in the 1975 World Series remains one of baseball's most iconic moments. Shown here is the front page of the *Boston Globe* the following morning, October 22. Fisk's career will always be highlighted with the image of him swinging and waving the ball fair before it bounced off the left field foul pole to win game six in dramatic fashion. (Courtesy of Ray Sinibaldi.)

At the hall of fame induction ceremony on July 23, 2000, Fisk and fellow inductee and former teammate Tony Perez proudly pose with the bronze plaques they had just been awarded. The two players competed against each other in the historic, hard-fought 1975 World Series and were teammates on the 1979 and 1980 Red Sox. They played a combined total of 47 seasons in the major leagues.

Shortly after he was inducted into the hall of fame, the Red Sox held a ceremony to retire Fisk's uniform No. 27. On September 4, 2000, he became the fifth Red Sox player so honored, joining Ted Williams, Joe Cronin, Bobby Doerr, and Carl Yastrzemski. As he walked around holding his framed number, he approached the left field foul pole to pay homage to the memory of his famous home run.

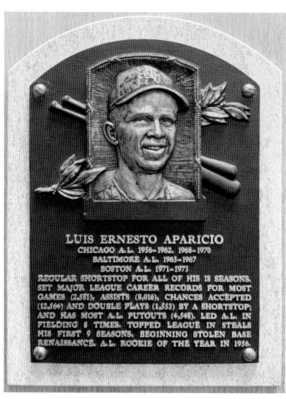

LUIS ERNESTO APARICIO
CHICAGO A.L. 1956-1962, 1968-1970
BALTIMORE A.L. 1963-1967
BOSTON A.L. 1971-1973
REGULAR SHORTSTOP FOR ALL OF HIS 18 SEASONS.
SET MAJOR LEAGUE CAREER RECORDS FOR MOST
GAMES (2,581), ASSISTS (8,016), CHANCES ACCEPTED
(12,564) AND DOUBLE PLAYS (1,553) BY A SHORTSTOP,
AND HAS MOST A.L. PUTOUTS (4,548). LED A.L. IN
FIELDING 8 TIMES. TOPPED LEAGUE IN STEALS
HIS FIRST 9 SEASONS, BEGINNING STOLEN BASE
RENAISSANCE. A.L. ROOKIE OF THE YEAR IN 1956.

The pride of Venezuela, Luis Aparicio burst upon the scene in 1956. He displayed spectacular defense at shortstop, led the American League in stolen bases, and won the Rookie of the Year Award. "Little Louie," pictured below with Orlando Cepeda, became the standard on defense at shortstop and won nine Gold Gloves. In 1970, at the age of 36, he had his best season offensively but was traded by the White Sox to Boston in December. Aparicio started off his career with the Red Sox with a seven-game hitting streak, including six runs batted in in his third game, and went to the All-Star Game for his 13th appearance. The first Venezuelan elected to the Baseball Hall of Fame, Aparicio had his 500th stolen base on July 5, 1973, against the Yankees. He was elected in 1984.

A NEW CAST OF LEGENDS

Plagued by knee troubles, Orlando Cepeda found himself without a team and his career appeared over following the 1972 season. His prospects changed when the American League adopted the designated hitter rule in January 1973, and one week later, the Red Sox signed him to fill that role. Cepeda was the National League's Rookie of the Year in 1958 and Most Valuable Player in 1967, and had slugged 358 home runs. Three months later, on opening day, he became the second player in history to come to the plate as a designated hitter, one inning after the Yankees' Ron Blomberg. Cepeda's first hit with Boston was a walk-off homer two days later, and he went on to hit 20 home runs that season on his way to becoming the first recipient of the Designated Hitter of the Year Award. He was elected in 1999.

In Juan Marichal's major-league debut in July 1960, he retired the first 19 batters he faced and carried a no-hitter into the eighth inning. After a highly distinguished career in the National League with 238 wins, a no-hitter, 10 All-Star selections, and the 1965 All-Star Game Most Valuable Player award, the "Dominican Dandy" was purchased by the Red Sox in December 1973. Marichal's best start with Boston came on August 11 against the world champion Athletics back in the Bay Area, home of his previous success with the San Francisco Giants. He won 2-1 with six strikeouts and allowed no earned runs. In 1983, Marichal was the first player from the Dominican Republic elected to the hall of fame.

A two-sport star in high school, South Carolina native Jim Rice had to choose between pro baseball and college football upon graduation. He was drafted in the first round by the Boston Red Sox and offered a football scholarship to Clemson University. Red Sox fans would be forever grateful he chose baseball. "Jim Ed," as he liked to be called, worked his way through the Boston system quickly and, after a tremendous season with Pawtucket in Triple A, was in the majors to stay by August 1974. Rice had a breakout season in 1975, finishing second to teammate Fred Lynn in Rookie of the Year balloting and third in the Most Valuable Player voting. One of the most feared hitters of his era, Rice's 1978 Most Valuable Player season is among the finest in Red Sox history. He was elected in 2009.

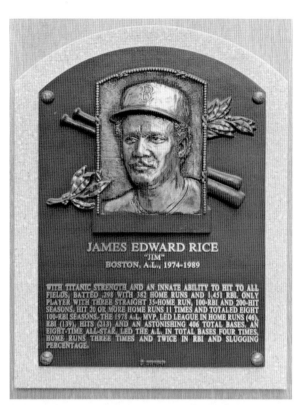

The Red Sox primary starting outfield from 1975 to 1980 consisted of, from left to right, Jim Rice, Fred Lynn, and Dwight Evans, seen standing in their respective positions. Over that six-season span, both Rice and Lynn won Most Valuable Player awards, the three were selected to 10 All-Star appearances, Lynn and Evans won a combined seven Gold Gloves, and the trio was considered the greatest outfield in baseball during that time.

On August 7, 1982, in one of the scariest moments to ever occur at Fenway Park, four-year-old Jonathan Keane was struck in the head by a foul ball. Jim Rice ran from the dugout, scooped up the unconscious, bleeding boy, and carried him into the clubhouse to waiting medical staff, who rushed him by ambulance to the hospital. Doctors later stated that Rice's quick, heroic action prevented permanent damage to the boy. (Courtesy of *Boston Herald*.)

A NEW CAST OF LEGENDS

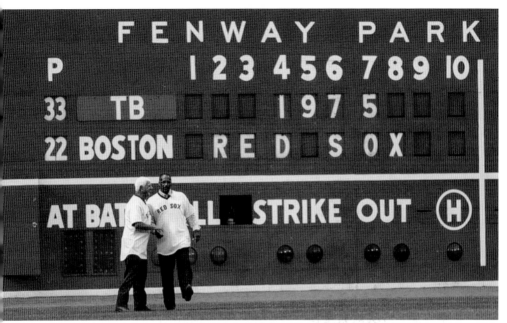

Rice is seen here with Carl Yastrzemski standing in front of Fenway Park's Green Monster. The pregame ceremony at Fenway honored the 40th anniversary of the Red Sox' pennant-winning 1975 season. Both men were big contributors to that memorable season, and fans will always be left to wonder how the outcome may have been different had Rice not broken his wrist late in the season. Pictured below is Ted Williams with Jim Rice early in Rice's career. In the 50 years from 1939 to 1988, these three hall-of-famers played 5,400 regular-season games in Fenway's left field as the torch was passed from Williams to Yastrzemski to Rice.

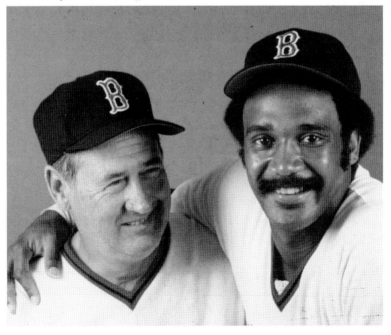

Twenty years after his final major-league game in 1989, Rice finally received the long-awaited call from Cooperstown. As the hall's newest member, he was given the VIP treatment, which included a tour of the museum. Here, Jim Ed is looking at a display case containing Red Sox memorabilia from 1975, his rookie year, and his own bat from his Most Valuable Player award-winning season of 1978.

In January 2009, the hall of fame held a press conference introducing its two newest members elected by the Baseball Writers Association of America, Jim Rice (right) and Rickey Henderson. When Henderson joined the Red Sox in 2002, he played many games in Rice's old position, continuing the left field hall-of-fame tradition at Fenway Park. Henderson and Rice proudly display their new bronze plaques at their induction.

A NEW CAST OF LEGENDS

Four weeks after Boston almost won the 1975 World Series, the team made a trade to add a quality starter, Fergie Jenkins. A seven-time 20-game winner, Jenkins still possessed excellent control and great durability. In his Red Sox debut on April 9, 1976, he pitched eight innings and allowed three hits, no walks, and one unearned run but was tagged with the loss. Ten days later, he threw his first of two shutouts that season. In all, Jenkins pitched 23 complete games in his two seasons with Boston, including a win on June 19, 1977, against the eventual world champion Yankees. His win-loss records in 1976 and 1977 do not do justice to the quality of his pitching while with the Red Sox. In 1991, Jenkins was the first native of Canada to be elected to the Baseball Hall of Fame.

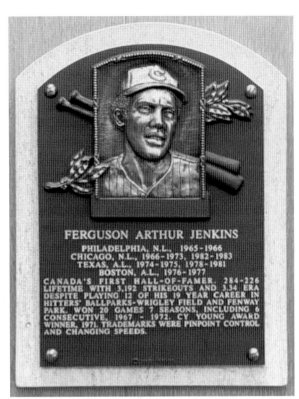

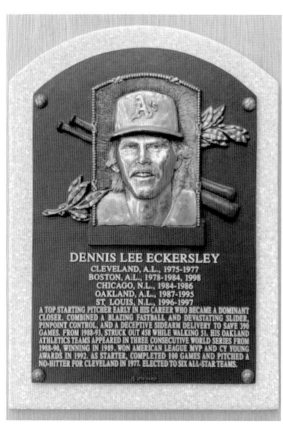

DENNIS LEE ECKERSLEY
CLEVELAND, A.L., 1975-1977
BOSTON, A.L., 1978-1984, 1998
CHICAGO, N.L., 1984-1986
OAKLAND, A.L., 1987-1995
ST. LOUIS, N.L., 1996-1997
A TOP STARTING PITCHER EARLY IN HIS CAREER WHO BECAME A DOMINANT
CLOSER. COMBINED A BLAZING FASTBALL AND DEVASTATING SLIDER,
PINPOINT CONTROL, AND A DECEPTIVE SIDEARM DELIVERY TO SAVE 390
GAMES. FROM 1988-93, STRUCK OUT 458 WHILE WALKING 51. HIS OAKLAND
ATHLETICS TEAMS APPEARED IN THREE CONSECUTIVE WORLD SERIES FROM
1988-90, WINNING IN 1989. WON AMERICAN LEAGUE MVP AND CY YOUNG
AWARDS IN 1992. AS STARTER, COMPLETED 100 GAMES AND PITCHED A
NO-HITTER FOR CLEVELAND IN 1977. ELECTED TO SIX ALL-STAR TEAMS.

Boston acquired 23-year-old pitcher Dennis Eckersley from Cleveland in March 1978. The trade paid immediate dividends, as the right-hander led the team in wins (20) and earned run average and went 11-1 at Fenway Park. He led the Sox in both categories again the following season and became a mainstay in the rotation for six seasons. Eckersley also pitched a one-hitter against Toronto in September 1980. In May 1984, he was traded to the Cubs for Bill Buckner, and he moved on to Oakland in 1987. Under Athletics manager Tony LaRussa, the course of his career changed forever when Eckersley was converted to a closer. The 1992 Cy Young Award winner returned to Boston for his final season in 1998. The 43-year-old sure-to-be hall-of-famer was used primarily in a setup role and made 50 appearances. He was elected in 2004. (Below, courtesy of Ray Sinibaldi.)

A NEW CAST OF LEGENDS

After 23 major-league seasons split between being a starting pitcher and a closer, Eckersley returned to the Red Sox for the 1998 season. He signed with Boston as a free agent in December 1997 and primarily served as a setup man for outstanding closer Tom Gordon. Eckersley succeeded in that role, helping Boston make it to the postseason while recording his 390th and final career save.

Settling in the Boston area after retiring as a player, Eckersley joined the New England Sports Network (NESN) in 2009 to provide color commentary on televised broadcasts of Red Sox games. He had previously done work in that field with the Turner Broadcasting System. "Eck" entertains viewers with his personal recollections of his career and colorful descriptions utilizing his own special lexicon. (Courtesy of NESN.)

ATANACIO PÉREZ RIGAL
"TONY"
CINCINNATI, N.L., 1964-1976, 1984-1986
MONTREAL, N.L., 1977-1979
BOSTON, A.L., 1980-1982
PHILADELPHIA, N.L., 1983

A CLUTCH PERFORMER THROUGHOUT AN ILLUSTRIOUS 23-YEAR
CAREER, HE TORMENTED THE OPPOSITION WITH HIS ABILITY TO
CONSISTENTLY DRIVE IN RUNS. HIS COMPOSURE UNDER PRESSURE LED
TO 379 HOME RUNS, 505 DOUBLES AND 1,652 RBI, INCLUDING SEVEN 100-
RBI SEASONS AND 954 RBI IN THE 1970s. A CATALYST OF CINCINNATI'S
TALENTED BIG RED MACHINE TEAMS DURING THE 1970s. HIS SUBTLE
LEADERSHIP AND TIMELY HITTING HELPED PACE THOSE CLUBS TO
FIVE DIVISION TITLES, FOUR PENNANTS AND TWO WORLD SERIES
CHAMPIONSHIPS.

Tony Perez spent the better part of the 1970s as a key member of Cincinnati's "Big Red Machine." In November 1979, after 16 major-league seasons, he signed as a free agent with the Boston Red Sox, his former foe in the 1975 World Series. Perez, seen below with Dwight Evans (left) the day he signed with Boston, became the starting first baseman for the Red Sox. Although 38 years old, Perez had a very productive season, with 25 home runs and 105 runs batted in, and reached several career milestones while with Boston. In 1981, he hit the 350th home run of his career and drove in his 1,500th run. On July 2, 1982, Perez swatted his 2,500th hit. He was elected in 2000.

As a high school baseball player in Tampa, Florida, Wade Boggs's approach to batting took a serious turn when he read *The Science of Hitting* by Ted Williams. He was selected in the 1976 amateur draft by the Red Sox, beginning a long journey through their minor-league system. Boggs made his debut with Boston in 1982 and finished third in the American League Rookie of the Year balloting. The following season, he established himself as one of the game's great hitters by winning the first of his five batting titles. He was so proficient at reaching base that he led the major leagues in on-base percentage every season from 1985 to 1989. After the 1985 season, Ted Williams was quoted as saying: "Boggs is as smart a hitter as I've ever seen." Boggs was elected in 2005.

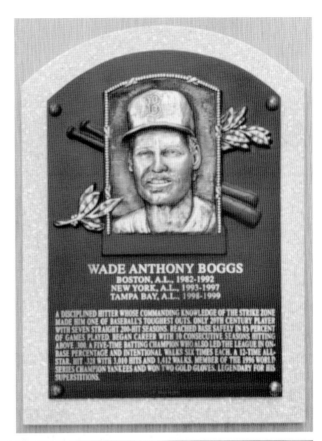

After four years of working his way through the Red Sox minor-league system, Boggs was finally promoted to the triple-A level in 1980. He spent two full seasons with the Pawtucket Red Sox in Rhode Island, just over the Massachusetts border. Aside from winning his league's batting title in 1981, Boggs was involved in the longest game in professional baseball history that spring, a 33-inning contest.

After his promotion to the majors, many questioned Boggs's defensive ability at third base. He worked diligently to improve his fielding and would go on to win two Gold Glove awards. He is third in most consecutive All-Star appearances as a third baseman with 12, behind only hall-of-fame legends Brooks Robinson and George Brett.

A NEW CAST OF LEGENDS

Wade Boggs at bat was a study in concentration, determination, and discipline. He was a student of the craft and elevated hitting to an artform. By his fifth season, he had established himself as the premier pure hitter in the game, and by the end of his first decade, he won five batting titles and six on-base percentage titles and had 1,965 hits, including 240 in 1985 to lead the major leagues.

Boggs joined an exclusive list of players from the Red Sox to have items from their careers displayed in the hall of fame's museum section. Shown here are the Franklin batting gloves that were used in the 1989 season, when he had his seventh straight 200-plus-hit season, an American League record at the time. Boggs finished his career with 3,010 hits and a .328 lifetime batting average.

Wade Boggs and Ryne Sandberg pose at a press conference upon the announcement of their election. Boggs and second baseman Sandberg (left) had been the dominant players at their respective positions in the 1980s and early 1990s. In his first year of eligibility, Boggs, also known as the "Chicken Man," led all players on the Hall of Fame ballot in 2005 by receiving 92 percent of the vote.

Eleven years after his induction into the hall of fame, the Red Sox formally took Boggs's uniform No. 26 out of circulation. One of the franchise's all-time great hitters, he joined eight other Red Sox players to have their number displayed on Fenway's right field facade. With his bronze hall plaque on display at the ceremony, Boggs told the crowd, "This is the final piece of my baseball puzzle."

A NEW CAST OF LEGENDS

Tom Seaver had accomplished everything a pitcher could hope for by 1986, having reached the milestones of 300 wins and 3,000 strikeouts plus a world championship and a no-hitter. He wanted to finish his career near his Connecticut home, so the White Sox traded him to Boston for Steve Lyons on June 29, 1986. The three-time Cy Young Award winner joined the pitching rotation and made numerous quality starts to help Boston win the American League East Division title. In his August 18 start in Minnesota, the 41-year-old allowed just three hits in his 311th and final career victory. A knee injury prevented him from pitching in the 1986 postseason, and the question still lingers whether he may have helped provide a different outcome in the World Series loss to the New York Mets. He was elected in 1992.

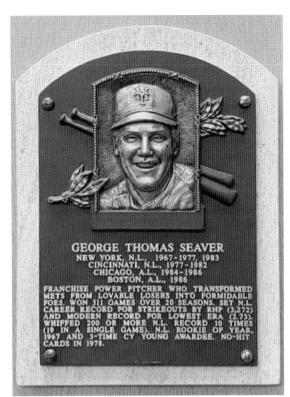

LEE ARTHUR SMITH

CHICAGO, N.L. 1980-87; BOSTON, A.L. 1988-90;
ST. LOUIS, N.L. 1990-93; NEW YORK, A.L. 1993;
BALTIMORE, A.L. 1994; CALIFORNIA, A.L. 1995-96;
CINCINNATI, N.L. 1996; MONTREAL, N.L. 1997

COMBINED BAT-SHATTERING FASTBALL AND DARTING SLIDER TO SAVE
478 GAMES, TOPPING THE ALL-TIME LIST FOR MORE THAN A DECADE.
ORIGINALLY A MULTI-INNING RELIEF ACE, TOTALED 169 SAVES OF
MORE THAN THREE OUTS. TRANSITIONED INTO FEARED ONE-INNING
CLOSER AS BULLPEN ROLES SPECIALIZED, BECOMING THE FIRST TO
RECORD AT LEAST 30 SAVES IN 10 DIFFERENT SEASONS. NAMED TO
SEVEN ALL-STAR TEAMS AND EARNED HIS LEAGUE'S RELIEVER OF THE
YEAR HONORS THREE TIMES. RETIRED WITH THE HIGHEST STRIKEOUT
RATE AMONG PITCHERS WITH AT LEAST 700 RELIEF APPEARANCES.

When the Red Sox acquired Lee Smith in December 1987, they filled a significant need with a closer who had been one of the best in the National League for the previous five seasons. Smith led his league in saves once and placed in the top five several other times. He was a big factor in Boston going from a fifth-place team the season before to the American League East champion. While closers were evolving into one-inning pitchers, the workhorse Smith had outings of two or more innings 14 times in 1988. He had another effective season in 1989 with 25 saves and was particularly tough on batters, striking out a lofty 12.2 per nine innings pitched. With his slow walk and intimidating glare, the 6-foot-5-inch, 250-pound Smith was the epitome of a dominating closer. He was elected in 2019. (Below, courtesy of Ray Sinibaldi.)

A NEW CAST OF LEGENDS

7

YAZ'S IMPOSSIBLE DREAM COMES TRUE

The son of a Long Island potato farmer, young Carl Yastrzemski grew up a Yankees fan. An outstanding high school player, he was scouted not only by the Yanks, but also by the Reds, Phillies, and Red Sox. During his senior year in high school, his dad and he journeyed to Yankee Stadium for a tryout, where young Yaz took but 10 swings and deposited four balls into the right field bleachers. Shortly thereafter, upon trying to sign young Carl, the elder Yastrzemski informed the Yankee scout at his table that he had set $100,000 as the minimum signing figure for his son. Upon hearing that demand, scout Ray Garland flipped a pencil up to the ceiling of the Yastrzemski kitchen in exasperation. The scout was shown the door by Yastrzemski Sr., and Yaz's dream of becoming a Yankee left with him.

After a year at Notre Dame on a baseball/basketball scholarship, he was signed by Boston scout "Bots" Nekola for a $108,000 bonus and spent 1959 playing second base in the minors. In February 1960, he was in spring training with the Red Sox and was given the locker next to Ted Williams. The two appeared in several games together, but management decided to send him down to their top minor league team in Minneapolis. They were fairly certain that Williams would retire after the 1960 season and wanted Yaz to spend that season learning to play left field and take over the position in 1961.

Yastrzemski adjusted well to left field and hit a robust .339 in 148 games with Minneapolis. Though there was considerable pressure on the 21-year-old, he was set to be the heir-apparent to the all-time legend. Yaz would say much later that after the expectations that came with replacing Williams, he never felt real pressure again.

While he did not match the accomplishments of "The Splendid Splinter," he arguably had the second-most noteworthy career in franchise history. In the end, he would conclude his career with well over 3,000 hits, more than 400 home runs, and a date with Cooperstown.

He is—as the song recorded about him in 1967 said—"The Man They Call Yaz."

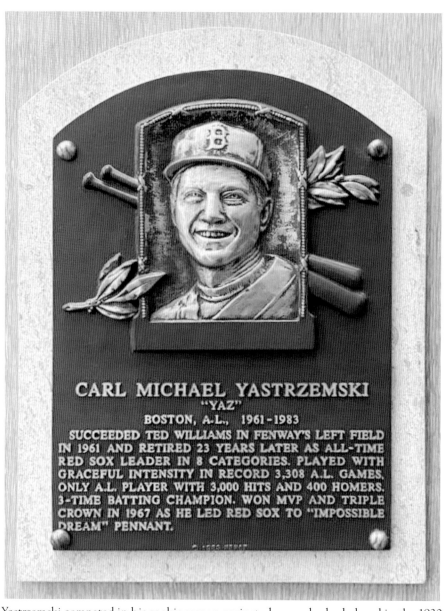

CARL MICHAEL YASTRZEMSKI
"YAZ"
BOSTON, A.L., 1961-1983
SUCCEEDED TED WILLIAMS IN FENWAY'S LEFT FIELD
IN 1961 AND RETIRED 23 YEARS LATER AS ALL-TIME
RED SOX LEADER IN 8 CATEGORIES. PLAYED WITH
GRACEFUL INTENSITY IN RECORD 3,308 A.L. GAMES.
ONLY A.L. PLAYER WITH 3,000 HITS AND 400 HOMERS.
3-TIME BATTING CHAMPION. WON MVP AND TRIPLE
CROWN IN 1967 AS HE LED RED SOX TO "IMPOSSIBLE
DREAM" PENNANT.

Carl Yastrzemski competed in his rookie season against players who had played in the 1930s and in his final year against players still active in the 21st century. The connections Carl Yastrzemski made with fellow players during his long career span nearly seven decades. In regular and postseason games, Yaz competed with or against 55 players and managers who ended up in Cooperstown. When Yastrzemski accomplished his amazing Triple Crown season in 1967, it was the third time a Red Sox player achieved the feat, which was not repeated for 45 years. After Yastrzemski recorded both his 3,000th hit and his 400th home run in 1979, his marks went unmatched for 21 years until Cal Ripken Jr. became only the second player in American League history to reach both milestones. When Cooperstown came calling, he sailed in with 95 percent of the vote in his first year of eligibility in 1989.

Yaz is pictured receiving batting tips from Ted Williams at spring training in Scottsdale, Arizona, in 1963. After his retirement as a player, Ted continued to attend Red Sox spring training to instruct the younger players. In his autobiography, Yastrzemski credited a session with Ted during his rookie 1961 season for helping him break out of a slump. Six months after this photograph was taken, Yaz won his first batting title.

Carl Yastrzemski learned to play outfield during his final season in the minors as he was being groomed to replace Ted Williams. Yaz, who had primarily been a second baseman in the minors, worked extremely hard and became an excellent defensive outfielder, mastering play of Fenway Park's left field wall. Over the course of his career, he was awarded seven Gold Gloves for outstanding defensive play.

Yastrzemski's historic 1967 season is universally regarded as his greatest of all. His American League batting title seasons of 1963 and 1968 are also often highlighted. Curiously overlooked are the quality seasons he posted in 1965 and 1970. In both years, Yaz led his league in on-base percentage and the on-base plus slugging metric, and was also second in batting average, missing the 1970 title by .0003.

After hitting a single in the 1967 World Series at Fenway Park, Yaz crosses paths with St. Louis Cardinals star first baseman Orlando Cepeda. Both players would win the Most Valuable Player award in their respective leagues that season, and the two became teammates on the Red Sox in 1973. They would reunite years later after Cepeda joined Yastrzemski in the hall of fame in 1999.

Six weeks after the Red Sox lost the 1967 World Series, Yaz had a chance to reflect on the magnitude of his historic season. Here he is at home with various awards from that year, including the American League's Most Valuable Player award, Batting Title, and Triple Crown. Yastrzemski also won the Major League Player of the Year and Sports Illustrated Sportsman of the Year Awards.

On April 8, 1975, the one-year anniversary of breaking Babe Ruth's home run record, Hank Aaron is standing on first base at Fenway Park with Yastrzemski. Aaron was acquired after the 1974 season by the Milwaukee Brewers to be their designated hitter after playing with the Braves for 21 seasons. Both hall-of-fame sluggers played 23 seasons, combining for 1,207 home runs and 7,190 hits.

A special moment in the career of Carl Michael Yastrzemski occurred on Yaz Day at Fenway Park, Saturday, October 1, 1983. In a pregame ceremony before his next-to-last game, he was presented with many gifts and gave an emotional speech. Afterward, Yastrzemski took a lap around the field giving high-fives to fans in the stands, whom he said later kept yelling "We love you Yaz!" (Courtesy of Ray Sinibaldi.)

Yaz stands on the podium to accept his induction into the hall of fame. In his eloquent speech, he admitted to not being blessed with the same God-given talent or physical strength as many of his peers, and he had to work twice as hard. He was extremely complimentary and appreciative of team owner Tom Yawkey and was very grateful to have spent his entire 23-year career in a Red Sox uniform.

In July 1989, four weeks shy of his 50th birthday, Yaz was inducted alongside three men he had crossed paths with at various junctures. Catcher Johnny Bench competed against him in the classic 1975 World Series, Red Schoendienst managed against the "Impossible Dream" Red Sox in the 1967 World Series, and umpire Al Barlick worked in that series.

The year after Yaz's induction, Rhode Island sculptor Armand Lamontagne's newly created statue of him was unveiled. The artist had previously sculpted likenesses of Babe Ruth, Ted Williams, Boston Celtics basketball star Larry Bird, and Boston Bruins hockey legend Bobby Orr. The Yaz statue has mainly been housed at Boston's Sports Museum of New England.

RED SOX IN THE HALL OF FAME

Two weeks after his enshrinement in Cooperstown, Yaz holds a frame with his No. 8 at a Fenway ceremony to retire his number, making him the fourth Red Sox player so honored. Below in 2013, thirty years after his emotion-filled final game at Fenway Park on October 2, 1983, a statue of Yaz was unveiled outside the park he called home for 23 seasons. Located near the park's Gate B, it depicts Yastrzemski as he waves to an adoring Fenway crowd just prior to stepping into the batter's box for the final time. In a pregame ceremony that day, Yaz threw out the first pitch to Red Sox designated hitter David Ortiz, who was five weeks away from leading the Red Sox to another World Series victory.

YAZ'S IMPOSSIBLE DREAM COMES TRUE

PEDRO LEADS
21st-CENTURY LINEUP

At the turn of the 21st century, the Boston Red Sox were one of the most successful and popular franchises in sports. Going to a Sox game was a generational rite of passage, and every game was sold out. But despite a legendary pedigree of hall-of-fame players, Red Sox Nation had not seen a world championship since 1918. Between 1919 and 2000, Boston made the playoffs nine times and the World Series four times, in 1946, 1967, 1975, and 1986. Each time, they lost in spectacular fashion four games to three.

Although fans continued to suffer through "the Curse of the Bambino," little did they know that big changes were on the horizon for their beloved Sox. In February 2002, a new ownership team took control, and the fortunes of Red Sox Nation turned virtually overnight. Rather than building a new stadium, the new owners renovated the tired and outdated Fenway Park and with it the culture of the team, turning the perennial also-rans into world champions again. With their newfound standard of expecting excellence, the Red Sox reached the American League Championship Series in 2003 only to lose to the dreaded Yankees in seven games, again in dramatic fashion. A new winning era had arrived in Boston, and the Red Sox captured their first World Series championship in 86 years, defeating the St. Louis Cardinals four games to none in 2004. The Red Sox appeared in the World Series again in 2007, 2013, and 2018, winning them all in dominating fashion. The curse was officially broken.

Since 2000, twelve new Red Sox players have been inducted into the Baseball Hall of Fame, and there is no doubt that a new cast will follow and continue the tradition.

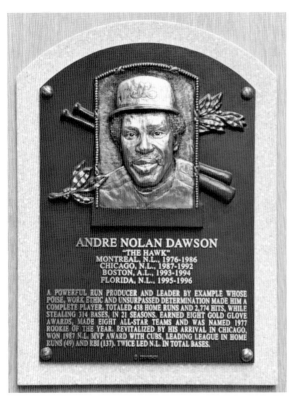

ANDRE NOLAN DAWSON
"THE HAWK"
MONTREAL, N.L., 1976-1986
CHICAGO, N.L., 1987-1992
BOSTON, A.L., 1993-1994
FLORIDA, N.L., 1995-1996

A POWERFUL RUN PRODUCER AND LEADER BY EXAMPLE WHOSE
POISE, WORK ETHIC AND UNSURPASSED DETERMINATION MADE HIM A
COMPLETE PLAYER. TOTALED 438 HOME RUNS AND 2,774 HITS, WHILE
STEALING 314 BASES, IN 21 SEASONS. EARNED EIGHT GOLD GLOVE
AWARDS, MADE EIGHT ALL-STAR TEAMS AND WAS NAMED 1977
ROOKIE OF THE YEAR. REVITALIZED BY HIS ARRIVAL IN CHICAGO,
WON 1987 N.L. MVP AWARD WITH CUBS, LEADING LEAGUE IN HOME
RUNS (49) AND RBI (137). TWICE LED N.L. IN TOTAL BASES.

Andre Dawson proved to be among the finest all-around players of his era. Signing with the Red Sox in December 1992, he brought with him 399 home runs, 2,504 hits, 319 stolen bases, 8 Gold Gloves, 8 All-Star selections, and both a National League Rookie of the Year Award and Most Valuable Player honor. By his mid-30s, he seemed on pace for the extremely exclusive 500–home run and 3,000-hit club, but 11 seasons playing on Montreal's artificial turf took a tremendous toll on his knees. Dawson's first home run with Boston was his 400th, surpassing Tigers legend and hall-of-famer Al Kaline. That home run allowed "Hawk," as he was known, to join Willie Mays as the only players in baseball history to have at least 400 home runs and 300 stolen bases. Dawson was elected in 2010.

The stolen base king played for nine different major-league teams over the course of his 25-season career, with the Red Sox being his next-to-last stop in 2002. When Rickey Henderson was signed as a free agent by Boston in February of that year, he brought with him exactly 3,000 hits as well as the all-time records for runs scored, walks, and stolen bases. On August 17, the 43-year-old had a very impressive day at the plate, going three for four with a home run and a double. Henderson successfully stole eight bases in 10 attempts and played his 3,000th game during his time with the Red Sox. On May 29, he stole two bases against the Toronto Blue Jays, the second of which was the 1,400th of his storied career. He was elected in 2009.

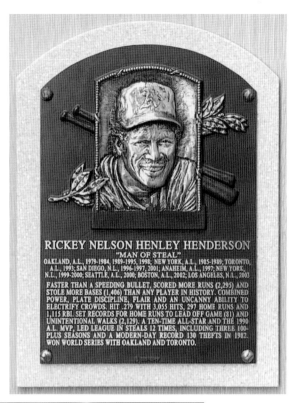

JOHN ANDREW SMOLTZ
ATLANTA, N.L. 1988-99, 2001-08; BOSTON, A.L. 2009;
ST. LOUIS, N.L. 2009

A WORKHORSE POWER PITCHER, TRADED HIS STARTING
DOMINANCE TO DEVELOP INTO PREMIER CLOSER BEFORE
RETURNING TO ROTATION, BECAME THE FIRST PLAYER IN
HISTORY WITH 200 WINS AND 150 SAVES, WITH A DYNAMIC
FASTBALL, A DECEPTIVE SLIDER AND A DARTING SPLITTER,
FANNED 3,084 BATTERS AND WAS NAMED TO EIGHT ALL-STAR
TEAMS. THE 1996 N.L. CY YOUNG AWARD WINNER AND 1992 NLCS
MVP, SET N.L. RECORD WITH 55 SAVES IN 2002. PITCHED BEST
WHEN GAME WAS BIGGEST, RECORDING A 15-4 POST-SEASON
RECORD, HELPING BRAVES TO 1995 WORLD SERIES TITLE.

After excelling as both a starting pitcher and a closer in the National League for 20 seasons, John Smoltz, an eight time All-Star, World Series champion, and 1995 Cy Young Award winner, brought his talents to the Red Sox and the American League in 2009. Smoltz became the first pitcher in history to be elected to the hall of fame after having Tommy John surgery and holds the rare distinction of having led his league in both wins and saves in different seasons. Becoming a relief pitcher after his surgery, Smoltz set the still-standing National League record for saves in a single season with 55 in 2002. Smoltz started several games for Boston in 2009 and was inducted alongside fellow Red Sox hall-of-famer Pedro Martinez in 2015.

PEDRO LEADS 21ST-CENTURY LINEUP

The Red Sox pulled off one of their most important trades of the late 20th century when they acquired pitcher Pedro Martinez in an extremely lopsided deal in November 1997. In his first season with Boston in 1998, he won 19 games and finished second in the American League in both earned run average and strikeouts. In 1999 and 2000, Pedro elevated his performance further, dominating the league with two of the most historic seasons of the 20th century for a pitcher on his way to winning the Cy Young Award in both seasons. His earned run average in 2000 was so much lower than the league average that it established a modern baseball record. Martinez played a big role in bringing Boston its first world championship in 86 years. His win-loss record in seven seasons with Boston was a remarkable 117-37. He was elected in 2015.

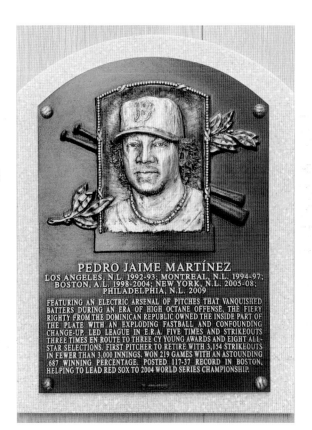

The historic 1999 All-Star Game was the third midsummer classic played at Fenway Park since the exhibition began in 1933. Pedro pitched the first two innings and struck out five of the six All-Stars he faced, including future hall-of-famers Barry Larkin, Larry Walker, and Jeff Bagwell. Martinez became the first pitcher to ever strike out the side to start an All-Star Game and was named the game's Most Valuable Player.

When the Red Sox acquired Pedro he had just completed a Cy Young Award–winning season in the National League. His successes continued in Boston and Martinez ran away with the American League Cy Young Award in both 1999 and 2000, which helped pave his road to Cooperstown. At that time, he joined Gaylord Perry and Randy Johnson as the only pitchers to have won the award in both leagues.

After yet another stellar performance, Pedro walks off the mound toward the Red Sox dugout to heartfelt cheers of an adoring, animated Fenway crowd. The always cheerful Pedro quickly became a beloved figure to Boston fans as they realized they were witnessing historic pitching exploits. An intense competitor, Martinez rewarded the local fans with a 58-18 pitching record at Fenway Park in his seven seasons calling the ballpark home.

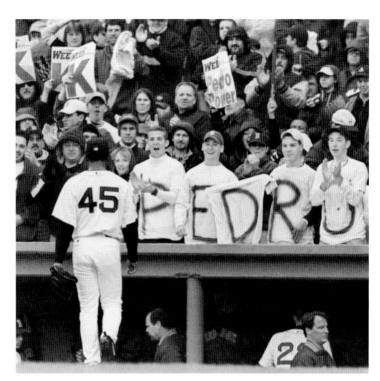

After 86 years, the Red Sox were finally able to celebrate a World Series victory on October 27, 2004. Pedro Martinez (left) and David Ortiz share a jubilant moment with the trophy during a celebration at Fenway Park years later. Martinez had won game three of the four-game sweep over St. Louis with no runs allowed over seven innings. Ortiz had a .582 batting average that postseason.

Here during 2000 is the perspective of a major-league hitter in the unenviable position of facing Pedro Martinez in the prime of his career. That season, he displayed a pitching dominance that was among the very finest in modern baseball history. Martinez ranked at the top of all American League pitchers that season in earned run average, strikeouts, shutouts, and fewest hits per nine innings pitched, among others.

At his hall of fame induction ceremony on July 26, 2015, Pedro shares a moment on the stage with Juan Marichal. As a youth growing up in the Dominican Republic, Martinez viewed his fellow countryman as an idol and a national hero. During his induction speech, Pedro invited Marichal to join him at the podium, and they displayed a Dominican flag to the delight of the crowd.

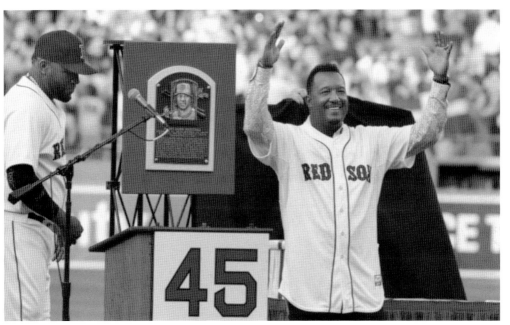

Just two days after being enshrined in Cooperstown, Pedro was honored by the Red Sox with the retirement of his uniform No. 45, joining the other numbers on Fenway's right field facade. At the ceremony, David Ortiz spoke glowingly of how great Pedro was as a teammate. Martinez told the adoring crowd, "As excited as I am about the hall of fame, I'm equally excited about having my number retired."

On January 25, 2022, the hall of fame announced that David Ortiz had been elected to take his place along the 45 members of the Red Sox family already enshrined. The journey ending in Cooperstown began when he came to Boston in 2003. Ortiz came through with countless clutch hitting performances, especially in the post-season. His .688 batting average in the 2013 World Series earned him Most Valuable Player honors.

When Ortiz, affectionately known as "Big Papi," appeared on the hall of fame ballot for the first time in late 2021, he had a virtual air-tight case for election. His 541 home runs, ten 100-plus RBI seasons, and contributions to three World Series championships made as strong a case for induction as one could hope for. The beloved Ortiz will always be adored for his emotional response after the 2013 Boston Marathon bombing.

Ortiz proudly displays four treasured pieces of jewelry he earned in his time with the Red Sox. Included are his world championship rings from 2004, 2007, and 2013, along with the ring he was awarded for being named the Most Valuable Player in the 2013 World Series. "Big Papi" was the first Red Sox player to contribute to three world championships in the 21st century.

PEDRO LEADS 21ST-CENTURY LINEUP

Ortiz had the shortest wait of any Red Sox player to have his number officially retired. Just eight and a half months after playing his final game in a Boston uniform, No. 34 joined nine other Red Sox numbers permanently set aside. Previous honorees Pedro Martinez, Wade Boggs, Jim Rice, and Carl Yastrzemski were on hand at the Fenway Park ceremony, held on June 23, 2017. Martinez had helped convince Red Sox management to sign Ortiz back in late 2002. Coming from the Minnesota Twins, Ortiz opted to wear No. 34 in honor of former player Kirby Puckett, whom he had idolized in his early years with the Twins. Below, upon his number retirement, a banner with Ortiz's name was added with other Red Sox greats on Van Ness Street, just outside Fenway Park. (Both, courtesy of Ray Sinibaldi.)

DISCOVER THOUSANDS OF LOCAL HISTORY BOOKS FEATURING MILLIONS OF VINTAGE IMAGES

Arcadia Publishing, the leading local history publisher in the United States, is committed to making history accessible and meaningful through publishing books that celebrate and preserve the heritage of America's people and places.

Find more books like this at
www.arcadiapublishing.com

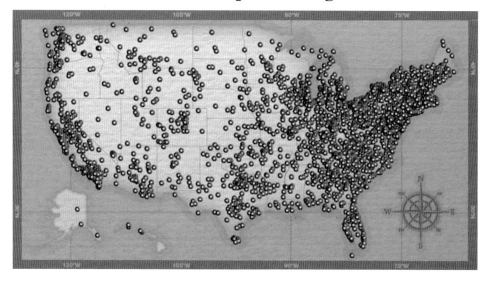

Search for your hometown history, your old stomping grounds, and even your favorite sports team.